Writing the Critical Essay

Bullying

An OPPOSING  VIEWPOINTS® Guide

Lauri S. Friedman, *Book Editor*

OPPOSING
VIEWPOINTS®
SERIES

GREENHAVEN PRESS
A part of Gale, Cengage Learning

 GALE
CENGAGE Learning

Detroit • New York • San Francisco • New Haven, Conn • Waterville, Maine • London

GALE
CENGAGE Learning˙

Christine Nasso, *Publisher*
Elizabeth Des Chenes, *Managing Editor*

© 2011 Greenhaven Press, a part of Gale, Cengage Learning

Gale and Greenhaven Press are registered trademarks used herein under license.

For more information, contact:
Greenhaven Press
27500 Drake Rd.
Farmington Hills, MI 48331-3535
Or you can visit our Internet site at gale.cengage.com

For product information and technology assistance, contact us at

Gale Customer Support, 1-800-877-4253
For permission to use material from this text or product, submit all requests online at
www.cengage.com/permissions

Further permissions questions can be e-mailed to permissionrequest@cengage.com

Articles in Greenhaven Press anthologies are often edited for length to meet page require-ments. In addition, original titles of these works are changed to clearly present the main thesis and to explicitly indicate the author's opinion. Every effort is made to ensure that Greenhaven Press accurately reflects the original intent of the authors. Every effort has been made to trace the owners of copyrighted material.

Cover image copyright © Helder Almeida, 2010. Used under license from Shutterstock.com.

LIBRARY OF CONGRESS CATALOGING-IN-PUBLICATION DATA

Bullying / Lauri S. Friedman, book editor.
    p. cm. -- (Writing the critical essay: an opposing viewpoints guide)
  Includes bibliographical references and index.
  ISBN 978-0-7377-5024-9 (hardcover)
  1. Bullying--United States. 2. Cyberbullying--United States. I.
Friedman, Lauri S.
  BF637.B85B842 2010
  302.3--dc22

                                          2010029207

Printed in the United States of America
1 2 3 4 5 6 7 14 13 12 11 10

CONTENTS

Examining the state of writing and how it is taught in the United States was the official purpose of the National Commission on Writing in America's Schools and Colleges. The commission, made up of teachers, school administrators, business leaders, and college and university presidents, released its first report in 2003. "Despite the best efforts of many educators," commissioners argued, "writing has not received the full attention it deserves." Among the findings of the commission was that most fourth-grade students spent less than three hours a week writing, that three-quarters of high school seniors never receive a writing assignment in their history or social studies classes, and that more than 50 percent of first-year students in college have problems writing error-free papers. The commission called for a "cultural sea change" that would increase the emphasis on writing for both elementary and secondary schools. These conclusions have made some educators realize that writing must be emphasized in the curriculum. As colleges are demanding an ever-higher level of writing proficiency from incoming students, schools must respond by making students more competent writers. In response to these concerns, the SAT, an influential standardized test used for college admissions, required an essay for the first time in 2005.

Books in the Writing the Critical Essay: An Opposing Viewpoints Guide series use the patented Opposing Viewpoints format to help students learn to organize ideas and arguments and to write essays using common critical writing techniques. Each book in the series focuses on a particular type of essay writing—including expository, persuasive, descriptive, and narrative—that students learn while being taught both the five-paragraph essay as well as longer pieces of writing that have an opinionated focus. These guides include everything necessary to help students research, outline, draft, edit, and ultimately write successful essays across the curriculum, including essays for the SAT.

Using Opposing Viewpoints

This series is inspired by and builds upon Greenhaven Press's acclaimed Opposing Viewpoints series. As in the parent series, each book in the Writing the Critical Essay series focuses on a timely and controversial social issue that provides lots of opportunities for creating thought-provoking essays. The first section of each volume begins with a brief introductory essay that provides context for the opposing viewpoints that follow. These articles are chosen for their accessibility and clearly stated views. The thesis of each article is made explicit in the article's title and is accentuated by its pairing with an opposing or alternative view. These essays are both models of persuasive writing techniques and valuable research material that students can mine to write their own informed essays. Guided reading and discussion questions help lead students to key ideas and writing techniques presented in the selections.

The second section of each book begins with a preface discussing the format of the essays and examining characteristics of the featured essay type. Model five-paragraph and longer essays then demonstrate that essay type. The essays are annotated so that key writing elements and techniques are pointed out to the student. Sequential, step-by-step exercises help students construct and refine thesis statements; organize material into outlines; analyze and try out writing techniques; write transitions, introductions, and conclusions; and incorporate quotations and other researched material. Ultimately, students construct their own compositions using the designated essay type.

The third section of each volume provides additional research material and writing prompts to help the student. Additional facts about the topic of the book serve as a convenient source of supporting material for essays. Other features help students go beyond the book for their research. Like other Greenhaven Press books, each book in the Writing the Critical Essay series includes bibliographic listings of relevant periodical articles, books, Web sites, and organizations to contact.

Writing the Critical Essay: An Opposing Viewpoints Guide will help students master essay techniques that can be used in any discipline.

Bullying: Not Just for Kids

Bullying is traditionally associated with school-yards and children, but emerging research shows that many adults never outgrow this age-old problem. Bullying is an issue for millions of adults in both real life and online, one that has worsened with the stress of the recession.

The Workplace Bullying Institute (WBI) collects data on the problem of workplace bullying and reports it is a significant problem in many American offices. In fact, the WBI has found that bullying is four times more common than illegal discriminatory harassment, such as sexual harassment or racial discrimination. More than a third of American workers—37 percent—have been bullied at work. That's an estimated 54 million Americans who deal with the problem. Bullies tend to hold positions of power. In fact, 72 percent of all workplace bullies are bosses or managers. Men bully more often than women, but women, when they do bully, pick predominantly on their female counterparts.

Workplace bullying takes many forms. Sometimes it reflects a competitive attempt to derail a colleague's chance of professional success or promotion. For example, a woman might bully a female colleague by limiting her access to important information about key meetings or committees; she might also steal or obfuscate information about critical assignments. Oftentimes the bullying is very subtle, even difficult to describe. "An eye roll, a glare, a dismissive snort—these are the tactics of the workplace bully," explains reporter Tara Parker-Pope. "They don't sound like much, but that's why they are so insidious. How do you complain to human resources that your boss is picking on you?"[1]

Researchers from the State University of New York and Wayne State University have identified more than twenty behaviors that, when demonstrated to the extreme and/or repetitively over time, constitute workplace bullying. These include being left out of work-related social events; being given the "silent treatment;" being the butt of rumors, pranks, or cruel jokes; being yelled at, unfairly criticized, or insulted; and being given shorter deadlines or bigger workloads than others. Sometimes, the bullying is downright juvenile. As reported by journalist Mickey Meese, "A private accountant in California said she recently joined a company and was immediately frozen out by two women working there. One even pushed her in the cafeteria during an argument, the accountant said. 'It's as if we're back in high school,' she said."[2]

In some cases, bullying is an outgrowth of stress brought on by the recession. In the United Kingdom, for example, where instances of bullying have doubled over the last decade, human resources and employment case managers say that as business has become more stressful and difficult, bosses, managers, business-owners, and colleagues have turned to bullying as a way to relieve their stress and compete with each other for dwindling positions. "The recession has become a playground for many bullies who know they can get away with it," says Lyn Witheridge, who recently ran a helpline for bullied workers. "Under pressure, budgets have got to be met. Managers are bullying people as a way of forcing them out and getting costs down."[3] Fraser Younson, head of employment at a prominent British law firm, agrees. "As running businesses has become more difficult, the way managers interface with their staff has become more demanding," he says. "Managers are chasing things up, being more critical. If they are not trained to deal with increased levels of stress, then we are seeing them do this in a way that makes staff feel bullied."[4]

Despite the prevalence of workplace bullying, it is often kept quiet: 62 percent of employers ignore the problem, 40 percent of those bullied do not report the problem, just 3 percent of those bullied file lawsuits about the matter, and 4 percent file a complaint with a state or federal agency. Because it is so underreported, the WBI has called bullying a "silent epidemic" that has profound emotional, physical, and professional consequences. Nearly half—45 percent—of those bullied report suffering from stress-related health problems such as anxiety, panic attacks, clinical depression, and even post-traumatic stress disorder. "In addition," reports the WBI, "once targeted, a person has a 64 percent chance of losing the job for no reason."[5] Even subtle bullying hurts victims' self-esteem and job performance. "Imagine yourself sitting at a conference table and you offer something as a suggestion and someone looks at you and shakes their head every time," says Joel H. Neuman, of the State University of New York–New Paltz School of Business. "It can be damaging to be constantly dismissed in front of your peers."[6]

Although the recession has been a cause of workplace bullying, it may also be the key to improving the problem. Bullying taxes workers' self-esteem and job performance and contributes to worker absenteeism and high turnover rates, all of which cost employers money. As such, employers are realizing it behooves them to cut down on bullying within their office walls.

Workplace bullying is just one of the issues explored in *Writing the Critical Essay: Bullying*. Readers will examine the extent to which bullying is an issue, whether it constitutes a rite of passage or a life-threatening problem, the phenomenon of cyberbullying, and whether laws against bullying negatively affect free speech. Model essays and thought-provoking writing exercises help readers write their own narrative essays on this important subject.

Notes

1. Tara Parker-Pope, "When the Bully Sits in the Next Cubicle," *New York Times*, March 25, 2008. www.ny times.com/2008/03/25/health/25well.html?em&ex = 12 06676800&en = 31b986ad49824972&ei = 5087%0A.

2. Mickey Meese, "Backlash: Women Bullying Women at Work," *New York Times*, May 10, 2009. www.ny times.com/2009/05/10/business/10women.html?page wanted = 1&_r = l.

3. Quoted in Afua Hirsch, "Bullying in the Workplace on the Rise," *Guardian* (Manchester), January 4, 2010. www .guardian.co.uk/money/2010/jan/04/bullying-work place-recession.

4. Quoted in Hirsch, "Bullying in the Workplace on the Rise."

5. "Results of the WBI U.S. Workplace Bullying Survey," Workplace Bullying Institute, August 2007. http://work placebullying.org/research/WBI-Zogby2007Survey .html.

6. Quoted in Parker-Pope, "When the Bully Sits in the Next Cubicle."

**Section One:
Opposing
Viewpoints
on Bullying**

Bullying Is a Life-Threatening Problem for American Children

Sirdeaner Lynn Walker

Sirdeaner Lynn Walker is the mother of Carl Walker-Hoover, an eleven-year-old boy who committed suicide after being bullied at school. Walker argues that relentless teasing, bullying, and mean-spiritedness drove her son to hang himself with an extension cord in his room. Walker says her son is not the only one who has been a serious target for bullies—bullying is a problem faced by countless children in American schools. Walker urges lawmakers and educators to adopt anti-bullying policies so that future children will not be bullied to death as was her son.

Consider the following questions:

1. What day did Carl Walker-Hoover commit suicide?
2. What steps does Walker say she took to protect her son from being bullied?
3. What is the National Day of Silence, according to Walker?

My name is Sirdeaner Lynn Walker, and four months ago I would not have dreamed that one day I would be testifying on Capitol Hill. I was an ordinary working mom, looking after my family and doing the best I could as a parent. But my life changed forever on April 6th, 2009. That night I was cooking dinner when my son, Carl Joseph Walker-Hoover, went to his room, where

Sirdeaner Lynn Walker, *Congressional Hearing Transcript Database*. Washington, DC: Federal News Service, 2009. Copyright © 2009 Federal News Service. Reproduced by permission.

I imagined he'd be doing his homework or playing his video games. Instead, I found him hanging by an extension cord tied around his neck. He was 11 years old.

Bullied to Death

Carl liked football and basketball and playing video games with his little brother. He loved the Lord, and he loved his family. What could make a child his age despair so much that he would take his own life? That question haunts me to this day, and I will probably never know the answer.

What we do know is that Carl was being bullied relentlessly at school. He had just started secondary school in September, and we had high hopes. But I knew something was wrong almost from the start. He didn't want to tell me what was bothering him, but I kept at him, and he finally told me.

Bullying can have devastating physical and emotional effects on its victims and can lead to suicide.

Bullying Behavior Chart

Bullying takes many forms, some more serious than others.

Physical Bullying - Harm to someone's body or property	
Level One	
Verbal	Expressing physical superiority, blaming the victim for starting the conflict.
Nonverbal	Making threatening gestures, defacing property, pushing/shoving, taking small items from others.
Level Two (some of these behaviors are against the law)	
Verbal	Threatening physical harm.
Nonverbal	Damaging property, stealing, starting fights, scratching or biting, pushing, tripping or causing a fall, assaulting.
Level Three (some of these behaviors are against the law)	
Verbal	Making repeated and/or graphic threats (harassing). Practicing extortion (such as taking lunch money). Threatening to keep someone silent: "If you tell, it will be a lot worse!"
Nonverbal	Destroying property, setting fires, physical cruelty, repeatedly acting in a violent, threatening manner. Assaulting with a weapon.

Emotional Bullying - Harm to someone's self-esteem or feeling of safety	
Level One	
Verbal	Insulting remarks, calling names, teasing about possessions, clothes, physical appearance.
Nonverbal	Giving dirty looks, holding nose or other insulting gestures.
Level Two (some of these behaviors are against the law)	
Verbal	Insulting family, harassing with phone calls. Insulting your size, intelligence, athletic ability, race, color, religion, ethnicity, gender, disability, or sexual orientation. Saying someone is related to a person considered an enemy of this country (e.g., Osama bin Laden).
Nonverbal	Defacing school work or other personal property, such as clothing, locker, or books.
Level Three (some of these behaviors are against the law)	
Verbal	Harassing you because of bias against your race, color, religion, ethnicity, gender, disability, or sexual orientation.
Nonverbal	Destroying personal property, such as clothing, books, jewelry. Writing graffiti with bias against your race, color, religion, ethnicity, gender, disability, or sexual orientation.

Social Bullying - Harm to someone's group acceptance	
Level One	
Verbal	Gossiping, starting or spreading rumors. Teasing publicly about clothes, looks, relationships with boys/girls, etc.
Nonverbal	Ignoring someone and excluding them from a group.
Level Two (some of these behaviors are against the law)	
Verbal	Harrassing using notes, Instant Messaging, Facebook, Twitter, e-mail, etc. Posting slander in public places (such as writing derogatory comments about someone in the school bathroom or online).
Nonverbal	Playing mean tricks to embarrass someone.
Level Three (some of these behaviors are against the law)	
Verbal	Enforcing total group exclusion against someone by threatening others if they do not comply.
Nonverbal	Arranging public humiliation either in person or online.

Taken from: US Department of Education, *Exploring the Nature and Prevention of Bullying.* Washington, DC: Office of Safe & Drug Free Schools.

The school—the kids at school were pushing him around, calling him names, saying he acted gay, and calling him faggot. Hearing that, my heart just broke, and I was furious. So I called the school right away, and I told them about the situation. I expected they would be just as upset as I was, but instead they told me it was just an ordinary social interaction and that it would work itself out. I desperately wish they had been right, but it just got worse.

I did everything that a parent is supposed to do. I chose a good school. I joined the PTO. I went to every parent teacher conference. I called the school regularly, and I brought the bullying problem to their staff's attention. The school did not act. The teachers did not know how to respond.

The Power of Words

"Sticks and stones can break your bones, but words can never hurt you." I have always hated that fable. Words do hurt. Words can kill.

Kymberly Foster Seabolt, "Words Can Be Deadly: Bullies Can Go Digital, Beyond the Classroom," *Farm and Dairy*, February 4, 2010. www.farmand dairy.com/columns/life-out-loud/words-can-be-deadly-bullies-can-go-digital-beyond-the-class room/14151.html.

Bullying Need Not Be Inevitable

After Carl died, I could've stayed home and mourned, but instead I've chosen to get involved, to speak out about school bullying. And I have learned in a short time that the most important thing I've learned is that bullying is not an inevitable part of growing up. It can be prevented, and there isn't a moment to lose.

Since my son died, I met the mother of another 11-year-old boy, who was also being seriously bullied and killed himself. And now—I know that there are others. This has got to stop. School bullying is a national crisis, and we need a national solution to deal with it. That is why I'm here today.

Educators need additional support and clear guidance about how to ensure that all our kids feel safe at school. Congress can make sure they have the guidance and support by making anti-bullying policies mandatory at all our nation's schools.

Every school should have one, and we shouldn't rest until they do.

We Cannot Afford to Wait

The Safe Schools Improvement Act would help achieve this goal, and it is supported by over 30 national education, health, religious and other organizations. I urge the subcommittees to move this legislation forward. We cannot afford to wait for another child to drop out of school, to struggle academically, or even worse, take his own life before we take this problem seriously.

Before I finish, I want to say one more thing. Very soon after Carl died, I heard from an organization called GLISTEN, which stands for Gay, Lesbian and Straight Education Network. They were offering their sympathy and support, and it meant a lot to me to learn that I wasn't alone, that other families had gone through this. But I have to admit I at first was very nervous.

My son was only 11 years old. He didn't identify as gay or straight or anything like that. He was a child. Those kids at his school called him those names because they were probably the most hurtful things they could think of to say, and they hit their mark. So I don't know what to expect when I—when my contact with GLISTEN brought me together with a diverse group of students, some of whom had been victims of bullying. It was the National Day of Silence, a day that gets young people involved in raising bullying—about bullying. They were kids from a wide range of backgrounds. And what amazed me the most was how much common ground we had. We shared our stories, and it gave me hope that the courage—and the courage to speak out on behalf of my son Carl.

Bullying Affects Us All

I know that bullying is not a gay issue or a straight issue. It's a safety issue. It's about what kind of learning envi-

ronment we want our children to have and how far we are willing to go to protect and teach them. That was the first day I started to believe we could do something about this problem. And believe it or not, that day would have been Carl's 12th birthday, on April 17th. I would like to think he rested just a little easier, knowing that all these brave young people are out there fighting for him and all the children like him.

So, in closing, I want to thank yon once again for the honor of this opportunity. I ask you to please do

School bullies create a safety issue for other students, which is why some suggest schools adopt mandatory anti-bullying policies.

everything—everything—in your power to make sure that no other family has to go through what my family went through. Please help us to stop school bullying. Please help our children—all of our children—who are suffering in our schools today. Thank you very much.

Analyze the essay:

1. This essay used narrative elements to make its point that bullying is a serious problem. Identify these narrative elements and explain whether or not you they helped convince you of the author's argument.

2. Walker says schools need to adopt anti-bullying policies to prevent bullying from taking place. If you were in charge of drafting such a policy, what would you suggest school administrators do? Use specific examples from your school. For example, if you know bullying is a problem at a specific time of day in a specific area of the school, you might suggest that area be closed during certain hours.

Most Bullying and Other Conflict Between Children Is Normal and Healthy

Helene Guldberg

In the following essay, Helene Guldberg argues that bullying is not a serious problem for most children. In fact, says Guldberg, much conflict between children is normal, healthy, and positively impacts their development. Guldberg says too often, anti-bullying campaigns encourage teachers, parents, administrators, and other authority figures to intervene in conflicts between children. But when this happens, children fail to learn to work problems out by themselves, and the conflicts tend to get blown out of proportion. Guldberg says only the very small minority of bullying cases require such intervention—the vast majority involve common nastiness and pettiness that can and should be handled between children. For all of these reasons, Guldberg concludes that most bullying is not serious and that children benefit from working out their problems among themselves.

Guldberg is the author of *Reclaiming Childhood: Freedom and Play in an Age of Fear*, where this essay was originally published. She is cofounder and director of *Spiked*, the first custom-built online current affairs publication in the United Kingdom.

Helene Guldberg, *Reclaiming Childhood: Freedom and Play in an Age of Fear*. Andover, Hampshire: Routledge, 2009. Copyright © 2009 Helene Guldberg. Reproduced by permission of the publisher.

Consider the following questions:
1. Why is it wrong to treat all instances of bullying as serious and life-threatening, according to Guldberg?
2. What does Guldberg say is the thrust of anti-bullying campaigns, and why does she view this as problematic?
3. Who is Benjamin Cox and how does he factor into the author's argument?

While some voices in recent years have spoken up to challenge the safety-first culture surrounding children today, drawing attention to the problem of raising a generation of cosseted, 'cotton wool' kids and arguing the need for children to be able to take more physical risks, one rarely hears any objection to the notion that children increasingly need to be protected from the 'emotional risks' posed to them by their peers in the form of bullying.

In this respect the old adage 'Sticks and stones may break my bones / But words will never hurt me' has been turned on its head. Some may concede that kids today could do with a few more broken bones, if this allows them the freedom to climb trees or play conkers; but the notion that children can be damaged for life as a result of insults hurled at them by their fellow pupils has become accepted as common sense. Consequently, the raft of behavioural codes that now regulate playground behaviour, and the increasingly interventionist role of adults in children's disputes, is seen as a necessary and humane development.

But the anti-bullying crusade has its own problems. The most serious is that children's relationships with other children are assumed to be damaging, and children are tacitly encouraged to look upon their peers with trepidation and suspicion. As more and more forms of behaviour are labelled as 'bullying' more and more children become labelled as 'bullies' or 'victims'.

Today children are pushed to look upon their everyday encounters with their friends or enemies through the prism of potential violence and abuse, and encouraged to seek help from teachers or other adults. This leads to a situation where children can become unwilling to, and incapable of, resolving their own problems with their peers: a process that damages children's development, and their relationships with each other, far more than the odd stone thrown or insult shouted.

Most Bullying Is Not Very Serious

For a minority of children, bullying is a profound problem. Each year we read tragic news stories of children taking their own lives after years of incessant bullying. In

Experiencing teasing or social isolation is a hurtful, yet normal childhood experience. Bullying can be a much more damaging experience.

2004 thirteen-year-old Laura Rhodes from Neath, South Wales, took a fatal overdose. Her parents said she had been terrified by the bullying and taunts she endured each day. The same year, twelve-year-old Aaron Armstrong was found hanged in a hayshed at the family farm in County Antrim in Ireland after being bullied at school.

In the 2007 book *Bullycide in America* a number of mothers tell the most painful stories of their lives—having watched their loved ones suffer and struggle because of bullying and eventually seeing no other way out but to end their short lives. The book is edited by Brenda High, who lost her thirteen-year-old son, Jared, to suicide in September 1998.

Such stories are heart-breaking: and that is why we need to put the discussion about bullying in its proper perspective. Much that is defined as bullying today is not bullying. It is boisterous banter or everyday playground disputes that could—and should—be resolved *without* adult intervention. Treating all playground disputes as serious acts of abuse does not help victims of terrible bullying, like Laura, Aaron and Jared. In fact it discourages a proper sense of vigilance about real brutality perpetrated by a handful of children, in favour of problematizing all relationships between all children. . . .

> # Adults Cannot Always Rescue Children
>
> Children are not always nice to each other, but people are not always nice to each other. The world is not like that. One of the things in danger of being lost is children spending time with other children out of sight of adults; growing a sense of consequence for their actions without someone leaping in.
>
> Tim Gill, quoted in Anushka Asthana, "Bullying Is Exaggerated, Says Childhood Expert," *Guardian/Observer*, October 28, 2007. www.guardian.co.uk/uk/2007/oct/28/schools.pupilbehaviour.

Not All Childhood Strife Counts as Bullying

The more broadly bullying is defined the more children could be described as being bullied. Someone having fun at someone else's expense, or being shunned by a group of friends, cannot feature too infrequently in most children's everyday lives. I am sure that my experience of at times being left out of certain friendship circles at school is not that uncommon—though I didn't define it as bullying then, and I wouldn't now. My family moved from Bergen to Trondheim when I was nine years of age and my siblings and I all went through the mortifying experience of being laughed at by other schoolkids because of our Bergen accent (which is quite unique, but charming, in my biased view). We all battled to get rid of our accents as quickly as possible. But although it was upsetting and frightening suddenly to be treated as an outsider, many of the same children later became good friends of ours.

Some childhood experiences are hurtful, and when you are a child a nasty taunt or a falling-out with your best friend genuinely does seem like the end of the world. That is very different, though, from the experience being harmful. Being left out of a playground game may make a child cry for a week, but by the following week it is likely to be involved again and all is forgotten. Children are not emotionally scarred by the experience; they get over it and move on. Once the experience is labelled as 'bullying', however, and a teacher becomes involved, it becomes an issue of much greater significance, driving a more permanent wedge between the putative victim and that week's bullies, and making it far harder for the spontaneous dynamics of playground life to resolve themselves.

Kids Must Learn to Resolve Their Own Disputes

The thrust of anti-bullying campaigns is to push teachers or other authority figures into children's conflicts on an everyday basis, in order to prevent 'bullying'. Such campaigns also push the message to children about the importance of telling somebody (i.e. a teacher, parent or other adult) if they are worried about bullying, either for their own sake or on behalf of a friend. But when bullying comes to mean anything that happens anywhere, this emphasis on involving a third (adult) party in a children's conflict is highly problematic. Throughout over a century of children's fiction, telling tales and running to teacher have stood as beacons of guidance about What Not To Do in terms of winning the respect of your peers and teaching bullies a lesson. Whether standing up to bullies involves a physical fight-back or another, cleverer strategy is immaterial. The point is that it has been well understood that what counts, above all, is children's ability to manage conflict themselves; after which point the conflict usually becomes resolved. If teachers become involved in every playground spat or squabble, it both blows the incident out of proportion and undermines the child's ability to manage the situation. . . .

There is a further danger with the notion that bullying can be anything, happening anywhere. If teachers are encouraged to see bullying in every childhood argument, they can easily lose the ability to see the wood for the trees. Truly debilitating bullying is thankfully rare, and this does need to be dealt with by adults, in a firm but sensitive manner. Yet if adults are encouraged to see just about any negative behaviour as bullying and to take action immediately, they could end up failing to act when a serious problem is staring them in the face.

Take the case of Benjamin Cox. In May 2007 a Supreme Court judge in Australia awarded eighteen-year-old Benjamin Cox $220,000, to be paid by the New South Wales Department of Education, for the pain and suffering he experienced as a result of being bullied. He was awarded a substantial additional sum for the economic loss that his trauma would cause him. Justice Carolyn Simpson said, 'He will never know the satisfaction of employment. He will suffer anxiety and depression for the rest of his life. He is unlikely to form any relationships. He has no friends and is unlikely to make any'.

Benjamin undoubtedly suffered at the hands of some rather nasty children. One incident—where a child had allegedly tried to strangle him—left him unconscious. Several months later he lost a tooth after the same child

Bullying Does Not Affect Most Kids

A survey of more than 1,200 boys and girls ages 9 to 13 found the majority of kids say bullying is not a problem for them: it happens only once in a while. When they are bullied, the majority of kids prefer to work out the problem among themselves.

Question: "How often have you been bullied?"

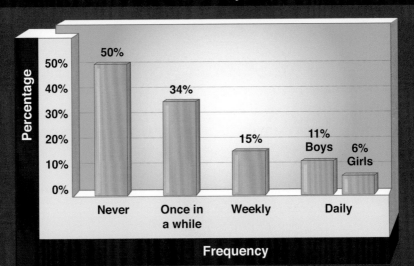

Question: "What do you usually do when someone bullies you?"

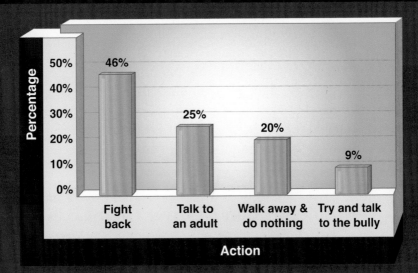

Taken from: KidsHealth Kids Poll, the Nemours Foundation/KidsHealth, the Department of Health Education and Recreation at Southern Illinois University–Carbondale, and the National Association of Health Education Centers.

Teachers who become involved in everyday playground spats can undermine the child's ability to fight back and earn the respect of his or her peers.

tried to ram his school jumper down his throat. Most parents would, quite understandably, be distraught if their child should face such a level of intimidation, knowing the fear and emotional pain that go with it, let alone the physical dangers. There are times when teachers clearly need to step in to reprimand children who are overstepping the mark, and in this case the school should surely have done something a lot earlier.

We Should Not Tell Children That Bullying Can Destroy Their Lives

Yet, even here, there is something worrying about Justice Simpson's statement that Benjamin will be damaged by the experience until the end of his days. Can it be right to tell an eighteen-year-old boy that his life is effectively over—that he 'will suffer anxiety and depression for the rest of his life' and 'is unlikely to form any relationships'? If adults talk about bullying as an experience that will blight the entire rest of their lives, children are less likely to find strategies to cope with and get over hurtful incidences. Although anti-bullying campaigns may have emerged out of concern for children's emotional welfare, they could end up projecting their own fears and insecurities on to children, and in the process making things worse.

The way children interpret events, and the emotional mark that these events leave on them, are very much shaped by the way adults respond to the events. Studies looking at the effect of early traumatic experiences on children's emotional development have found that neither the severity of the event nor the age of the child at the time can help us predict whether the child will experience behavioural or emotional problems later on. As child development expert Rudolph Schaffer points out:

> It has become apparent that there is no direct relationship between age and the impact [of] experience on the individual, that young children are not necessarily more vulnerable even to quite severe adversities than older children, and that considerable variability exists in long-term outcome.

The one variable that does seem to help predict the impact of traumatic events on later development is how the adults cope with the situation. If an adult breaks down and seems unable to comprehend what is going on, it is likely to have a detrimental impact on the children in his or her care.

So if the message to children who are being bullied is 'When bad things happen to you, your life could be destroyed for ever' could this response not be more damaging to children in the long term than the bullying itself? If we treat children as if they could not possibly cope with hurtful experiences, we are more likely to undermine their confidence and make them less likely to cope with difficult events in the future. . . .

Children Need to Work Out Disputes Among Themselves

Through unsupervised play children are given the opportunity to acquire skills such as co-operation and competition that are mainly learned through interactions with equals. Unless children are given the opportunity to engage with each other without adults hovering over them they won't really learn the consequences of being clumsy, nasty or thoughtless, or how to cope with good-natured teasing or spiteful and hurtful behaviour.

Children are, of course, much less sophisticated than adults. But it is precisely for that reason that they need to be given the opportunity to create and resolve conflicts. Playing, fighting and stumbling into difficult situations— the very things adults rush to stop—help shape children into competent and independent-minded individuals.

At times, in play, children test society's codes—they may push the boundaries of what is seen as acceptable behaviour. It is understandable that adults want to intervene when they feel children are misbehaving, but it may not necessarily be the best thing to do. Of course adults need to set some boundaries. When a child is clearly being scared witless by other children, adult intervention is necessary. But the boundaries need to be very carefully drawn and applied if the benefits of play are not to be undermined.

An Important Life Lesson

Unsupervised play isn't just some kind of childhood luxury that kids can do without. It is vital for children's healthy emotional and social development. We do children no favours by protecting them from all those experiences that may be distressing, or even risky, and that come with everyday life. But we would do them a real favour by expecting more of them and gently easing them into living life to the full—even if it entails getting some emotional or physical bruises along the way.

Analyze the essay:

1. Guldberg discusses the phenomenon of "bullycide" in which teens are driven to commit suicide after being bullied. What is Guldberg's take on bullycide? How does her opinion of it compare with Sirdeaner Lynn Walker's, author of the previous essay? After discussing both authors' positions, state with which you agree on how prevalent and serious the problem of bullycide is.

2. Guldberg believes that children learn important skills when they are left to work problems out by themselves. Consider the kinds of problems you have encountered with other students at your school. Did you, or would you have, benefited from going to an authority figure for help? Or, did you, or would you have, gotten more out of handling the problem on your own? Use specific details in your answer.

Cyberbullying Is a Serious Problem

Ashley Surdin

In the following essay, Ashley Surdin reports on the growing problem of cyberbullying. She explains that cyberbullying—harassment of a person via the Internet, cell phones, or other digital devices—is a growing and deadly phenomenon. Some children have committed suicide after being relentlessly harassed, while others have been driven out of their schools. Surdin says cyberbullying is particularly dangerous because the bullies have the advantage of remaining anonymous; children who would not normally bully someone to his or her face are willing to do so online where they can post mean and nasty comments anonymously. Surdin reports that several states have passed laws requiring schools to adopt anti-cyberbullying policies because the problem has worsened.

Surdin is a staff writer for the *Washington Post*, where this essay was originally published.

Consider the following questions:

1. What do Ryan Halligan and Megan Meier have in common, according to the author?
2. How many states does Surdin say have passed laws aimed at reducing cyberbullying?
3. Which age and gender group does Surdin say is most likely to be cyberbullied?

I n California, a hateful Internet campaign followed sixth-grader Olivia Gardner through three schools. In Vermont, a humiliated Ryan Halligan, 13, took his own life after being encouraged to do so by one of his middle-

Ashley Surdin, "In Several States, a Push to Stem Cyber-Bullying: Most of the Laws Focus on Schools," *The Washington Post*, January 1, 2009. Copyright © 2009, The Washington Post. Reprinted with permission.

school peers. And in perhaps the most notorious case, Lori Drew, 49, was convicted on misdemeanor charges for posing as a teenage boy on MySpace to woo and then reject 13-year-old Megan Meier of Missouri, who later hanged herself in her closet.

Such are a few of the anguished stories of cyber-bullying that are increasingly cropping up around the country, as more and more children and teenagers wage war with one another on computers and cellphones. The phenomenon has led to a push among states to

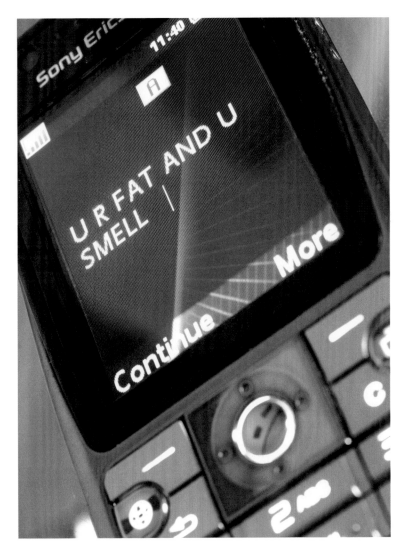

Children and teenagers are increasingly waging wars with each other on their computers and cell phones.

pass laws aimed at clamping down on the student-spun harassment, intimidation and threats coursing through the Web.

Making Cyber-Bullying Against the Law

Most of the laws are aimed at school districts, requiring them to develop policies on cyber-bullying—for example, how to train school staff members or discipline students. At least 13 states have passed such laws, including Arkansas, Delaware, Idaho, Iowa, Michigan, Minnesota, Nebraska, New Jersey, Oklahoma, Oregon, South Carolina and Washington. A handful of other states are considering similar measures.

This week, [January 2009] California becomes the latest state to tackle the issue. Starting today, California schools may suspend or expel students who commit cyber-bullying. The law also singles out such harassment as a subject to be addressed by school officials.

"This is part of a trend that is happening across the country, which is basically state legislatures telling the school districts that this is an issue they want them to address," said Nancy Willard, executive director of the Center for Safe and Responsible Internet Use, an Oregon-based organization that provides research and outreach for parents, educators and policymakers on Internet safety. "The message is: Do something."

No Refuge from Cyberbullying

This type of bullying can be more serious than conventional bullying. At least with conventional bullying the victim is left alone on evenings and weekends. . . . Victims of internet bullying, or cyberbullying, have no refuge. Victims may be harassed continuously via SMS [cell phone text messaging] and websites, and the information spreads very quickly and may be difficult to remove. In addition, it is often difficult to identify the perpetrator.

Ann Frisén, quoted in University of Gothenburg, "Cyberbullying: A Growing Problem," *Science Daily*, February 22, 2010. www.sciencedaily.com/releases/2010/02/100222104939.htm.

Challenges Abound

Though many schools throughout the nation have developed their own policies, some remain unsure how to handle cyber-bullying. It can be time-consuming and difficult

to investigate, given the veil of anonymity the Web offers. Educators may not understand the technology that students are using.

But the biggest cause of schools' hesitation, educators and legal experts say, is the fine line between protecting students from harassment and observing their right to free speech. That, Willard said, impels some educators to take a "not my problem" approach to off-campus cyber-bullying.

According to critics of the cyber-bullying laws, that's the right approach.

"The problem with these laws is that schools are now trying to control what students say outside of school. And that's wrong," said Aden Fine, a senior staff lawyer with the national legal department of the American Civil Liberties Union, which has closely followed such

Cyberbullying victim Ryan Halligan's father, John Halligan, raises awareness by sharing the events that led to Ryan's suicide.

legislation. "What students say outside of school—that's for parents to deal with or other government bodies to deal with.

"We have to keep in mind this is free speech we're talking about."

Willard said it is a mistake for school officials not to pay attention to cyber-bullying outside of school because escalating harassment often spills onto campus. Research also shows that such bullying leads to students' failing in school, avoiding class and contemplating suicide, she said.

As it is, schools may discipline students for actions outside of class if they disrupt the educational process, said Kim Croyle, a West Virginia lawyer who represents several school boards and lectures nationally on cyber-bullying. If, for instance, a student calls in a bomb threat from outside school or threatens another student so badly that they avoid school, the school could take action.

The real thrust of the state cyber-bullying laws, Croyle said, is setting a clear expectation for students and educators. "It takes a lot of the guesswork out," she said.

Cyber-Bullying Affects Nearly Half of All Teens

Cyber-bullying occurs when a minor is targeted in some form—threatened, humiliated, harassed—by another, and it is not to be confused with cyber-stalking or cyber-harassment, which involves an adult. Not limited to the Internet, cyber-bullying can spread by cellphones or other digital devices.

Four in 10 teenagers report that they have experienced some form of cyber-bullying, according to a 2006 study commissioned by the National Crime Prevention Council. It is more common among females than males, and most prevalent among 15- and 16-year-olds, according to the study.

Champions and critics of the laws agree that preventive education is a more powerful deterrent to cyber-bullying than discipline. That notion is supported by Patricia Agatston, co-author of "Cyber Bullying: Bullying in the Digital Age" and a counselor at Cobb County School District's Prevention-Intervention Center in Georgia.

"A lot of it can be prevented if we can just teach kids to think before they put things out there," Agatston said.

John Halligan, whose son Ryan took his life in Essex Junction, Vt., after many years of bullying, some online, applauded the national movement to enact cyber-bullying laws. But, he said, laws alone cannot stop the problem.

"I don't think a law would have prevented what happened here, quite frankly," said Halligan, who spends his time telling his son's story to schools.

"Even though what happened to Ryan happened online as well, it really started in school. I think that's the first step that a lot of states are missing."

Do Social Networks Facilitate Cyberbullying?

Students are more likely to be cyberbullied if they use a social network such as MySpace or Facebook.

Have you, personally, ever experienced any of the following things online?	Social Network User	Non-Social Network User
Someone taking a private email, IM, or text message you sent them and forwarding it to someone else or posting it where others could see it	17%	12%
Someone spreading a rumor about you online	16%	8%
Someone sending you a threatening or aggressive email, IM, or text message	16%	8%
Someone posting an embarrassing picture of you online without your permission	9%	2%
At least one of the forms of cyberbullying listed above	39%	23%

Taken from: Pew Internet & American Life Project Parents and Teens Survey, October–November 2006.

Analyze the essay:

1. Surdin discusses how some people have complained that anti-cyberbullying laws violate a person's right to free speech. What do you think? What is the difference between cyberbullying and free speech? Where does one end and the other begin? Offer specific examples in your answer.

2. Surdin explains that cyberbullying is especially problematic because children who would not normally bully someone to their face are willing to do so online where they can post mean and nasty comments anonymously. Think about how you use the Internet. Have you ever written something about someone online that you would not say to their face? If so, what empowered you to do so? If not, have you ever been the victim of such an attack? How did it feel?

The Problem of Cyberbullying Has Been Exaggerated

Larry Magid

In the following essay Larry Magid argues that cyberbullying is not as serious a problem as the media has made it out to be. He explains that most cases of cyberbullying are minor and typical; where cyberbullying has resulted in a death or a suicide, there were usually other contributing factors, such as depression or family troubles. Furthermore, Magid says that although the media has described cyberbullying as a rising epidemic, it is unclear how many teens have actually experienced it. For example, he says some surveys show as many as 80 percent of online youth have experienced cyberbullying, while other surveys show as little as 19 percent have. With such little consensus on cyberbullying, Magid says it is impossible to truly describe it as an epidemic. Magid says solutions exist to the problem of cyberbullying, and parents and educators need to think calmly and rationally about the problem.

Magid is a technology journalist and an Internet safety advocate.

Consider the following questions:

1. Who is Megan Meier and how does she factor into the author's argument?
2. According to Magid, what did a 2008 study by UCLA find about cyberbullying?
3. How does Magid say Aaron Hansen, the principal of White Pine Middle School in Ely, Nevada, reduces cyberbullying at his school?

The first things you need to know about cyberbullying are that it's not an epidemic and it's not killing our children. Yes, it's probably one of the more widespread youth risks on the Internet and yes there are some well publicized cases of cyberbullying victims who have committed suicide, but let's look at this in context.

Most Cyberbullying Is Not Life-Threatening

Bullying has always been a problem among adolescents and, sadly, so has suicide. In the few known cases of suicide after cyberbullying, there are other contributing factors. That's not to diminish the tragedy or suggest that the cyberbullying didn't play a role but—as with all online youth risk, we need to look at what else was going on in the child's life. Even when a suicide or other tragic event doesn't occur, cyberbullying is often accompanied by a pattern of offline bullying and sometimes there are other issues including long-term depression, problems at home, and self-esteem issues. And the most famous case of "cyberbullying"—the tragic suicide of 13-year-old Megan Meier—was far from typical. Cyberbullying is almost always peer to peer, but this was a case of an adult (the mom of one of Megan's peers) being accused of seeking revenge on a child who had allegedly bullied her own child.

And, as per "epidemic," it depends on how you define cyberbullying.

The most commonly recognized definition of bullying includes repeated, unwanted aggressive behavior over a period of time with an imbalance of power between the bully and the victim. In theory, that also covers cyberbullying, but some have taken a broader approach to cyberbullying to also include single or occasional episodes of a person insulting another person online. Indeed, because of the possibility of it being forwarded, a single episode of online harassment can have long-term consequences. "'Power' and 'repetition' may be manifested a bit differently online than in traditional bullying, Susan Limber, professor of psychology at Clemson University, said in an interview that appeared in a publication of the U.S. Department of Education's Office of Safe and Drug-Free Schools. She added, "a student willing to abuse technology can easily wield great power over his or her target just by having the ability to reach a large audience, and often by hiding his or her identity."

Manifestations of cyberbullying include name calling, sending embarrassing pictures, sharing personal information or secrets without permission, and spreading rumors. It can also include trickery, exclusion, and impersonation.

Fuzzy Numbers
Partly because there is no single accepted definition of cyberbullying, the extent of the problem is all over the

A cyberbully easily gains power over a victim because the Internet offers the bully the opportunity to reach a large audience.

map. I've seen some reports claim that up to 80 percent of online youth have experienced cyberbullying, while two national studies have put the percentage closer to one-third. A UCLA study conducted in 2008 found that 41 percent of teens surveyed reported between one and three online bullying incidents over the course of a year.

A recent study by Cox Communications came up with lower numbers, finding that approximately 19 percent of teens say they've been cyberbullied online or via text message and 10 percent say they've cyberbullied someone else.

One thing we know about cyberbullying is that it's often associated with real-world bullying. The UCLA study found that 85 percent of those bullied online were also bullied at school. . . .

Cyberbullying Can Be Prevented

After struggling with a school-wide bullying problem, Aaron Hansen, principal of White Pine Middle School in Ely, Nev., told Fox News that he asked the kids to fill out a survey indicating when the bullying took place and who the bullies were. He then invited the alleged offenders into his office to tell them "your peers feel that like you're not very nice to people at times and they feel like sometimes you're a bully." Based on working with those kids and working with their needs—including problems at home—the school was able to reduce the problem.

Not every situation will resolve itself quite so easily, but identifying the reasons kids are acting as bullies can

Cyberbullying Can Be Blocked or Ignored

There has been a lot of attention paid to the damage cyberbullying can do . . . but just as it can be meaner than bullying in person, it can also be easier to block or ignore. . . . Harris Interactive and The National Crime Prevention Council teamed up for research on cyberbullying and found that while it is happening (43 percent of the students they interviewed reported having been 'cyberbullied' in the past year), 61 percent of males and 52 percent of females said they were 'not bothered by it.' Teens view this issue as something that can be controlled by either just not responding, blocking the bully or through moderators intervening online. To them, it's not an issue schools should be addressing.

Anastasia Goodstein, "Most Teens 'Not Bothered' by Cyberbullying," *Totally Wired*, May 2, 2007. http://totallywired.ypulse.com/archives/2007/05/most_teens_not_bothered_by_cyb_1.php.

The suicide of Megan Meier (pictured here in images held by her mother) was a very unique cyberbullying case because she was harassed by an adult seeking revenge for her own child.

go a long way toward preventing it as can educational programs that stress ethics and cyber citizenship ("neti-quette"). It also helps kids to know what to do if they are victims of bullying. At ConnectSafely.org (a site I help operate) we came up with a number of tips including: don't respond, don't retaliate; talk to a trusted adult;

and save the evidence. We also advise young people to be civil toward others and not to be bullies themselves. Finally, "be a friend, not a bystander." Don't forward mean messages and let bullies know that their actions are not cool.

If your child is a victim of cyberbullying, don't start by taking away his or her Internet privileges. That's one reason kids often don't talk about Net-related problems with parents. Instead, try to get your child to calmly explain what has happened. If possible, talk with the parents of the other kids involved and, if necessary, involve school authorities. If the impact of the bullying spills over to school (as it usually does), the school has a right to intervene.

Beware of Anti-Cyberbullying Laws

There are lots of state laws that focus on cyberbullying, some requiring schools to provide educational resources. While I'm all for education, I think we need to be careful about any legislation that outlaws cyberbullying. U.S. Rep. Linda Sanchez (D-Calif.) has proposed H.R. 1966, well meaning legislation that could imprison for up to two years, "whoever transmits in interstate or foreign commerce any communication, with the intent to coerce, intimidate, harass, or cause substantial emotional distress to a person, using electronic means to support severe, repeated, and hostile behavior." On the surface, it seems fine but as UCLA law professor Eugene Volokh has pointed out, it could also be used to punish political and other forms of speech. "I try to coerce a politician into voting a particular way, by repeatedly blogging (using a hostile tone)," he writes, "I am transmitting in interstate commerce a communication with the intent to coerce using electronic means (a blog) 'to support severe, repeated, and hostile behavior.'" Professor Volokh said that if the law is passed, he expects it to be "struck down as facially overbroad."

Analyze the essay:

1. To make his argument that the problem of cyberbullying has been exaggerated, Magid claims that where cyberbullying cases have turned deadly, there were other factors at play. How do you think the other authors represented in this section would respond to that claim? Write one to two sentences per author. Then, state your opinion on what role cyberbullying played in the deaths Magid discusses.

2. Magid characterizes cyberbullying as simply the newest manifestation of an age-old problem. Do you agree? Or do you think something about cyberbullying is more dangerous than traditional schoolyard bullying? Explain your reasoning.

Laws Are Needed to Make Cyberbullying a Crime

Linda Sanchez

Linda Sanchez is a Democratic congresswoman from California. In the following essay, she argues that cyberbullying should be treated as a crime punishable by law. She discusses how there are grave consequences for the victims of cyberbullying—some of them have ended up dead after being tormented online. Yet under the law, there are no consequences for cyberbullies. Sanchez thinks cyberbullying should be treated as a criminal act because of the toll it takes on young peoples' self-esteem and their mental and physical health. Sanchez thinks that making cyberbullying against the law would not violate free speech because threatening people—whether in person or over the Internet—is not a constitutionally protected form of expression. She concludes that because it can have such serious consequences, law enforcement officials should be able to prosecute cyberbullies under the law.

Consider the following questions:

1. What actions does Sanchez point out as being against the law both online and offline?
2. What did a study by the United States Secret Service find about bullying, according to Sanchez?
3. What does Sanchez say the Supreme Court has recognized about reasonable regulation of speech?

Linda Sanchez, "Protecting Victims, Preserving Freedoms," HuffingtonPost.com, May 6, 2009. Reproduced by permission of the author.

If you were walking down the street and saw someone harassing a child, would you just walk by and look the other way? If that person was telling the child the world would be better off if they just killed themselves, would you ignore it?

This is what is happening on the internet except it is more painful, and can be more abusive because of the faceless anonymity the web provides. Bullies are using technology in ways we could not have imagined only years ago, and studies show that outdated and erroneous beliefs that bullying is "harmless" downplay its true seriousness.

Cyberbullying Deserves to Be Criminalized

Laws criminalize similar behavior when it takes place in person, but not online. In fact, we have laws criminalizing stalking, sexual harassment, identity theft and more when

Victims of repeated, severe, and hostile cyberbullying are put at risk for suicide and depression.

it takes place in person and online. All of these actions have consequences. But there is one serious online offense that has no penalty—cyberbullying. Do we not think it is as serious because it takes place in cyberspace and not face to face?

Missouri already has a law that criminalizes cyberbullying, but cyberbullying isn't just happening in one state. It's happening everywhere and it follows kids home—occurring at any hour of the day or night. Cyberbullying is hurtful enough and affecting kids enough that its victims have turned to suicide or violence just to make it stop. Should we just ignore it? Pass it off as simple child's play?

When so-called child's play turns hostile and a child becomes a victim, it is time to act. Victims of cyberbullying do not choose to participate. Rather than build character, bullying can cause children to become anxious, fearful, unhappy, and even cause them to be physically sick. A young person exposed to repeated, severe and hostile bullying online is deserving of protections because bullying puts them at risk for depression and suicide. According to a study by the United States Secret Service, being bullied is a risk factor for perpetrators of school violence, such as the kind that was unleashed with tragic results at Columbine High School in Colorado.[1]

We Should Not Tolerate Emotional Abuse
When so-called free speech leads to bullies having free-rein to threaten kids, it is time to act. The Supreme Court recognizes that in some instances words can be harmful.

> ## Some Laws Are Better than No Laws
>
> Laws are made to state the standards to which we aspire and to diminish people's ability to harm others as much as possible. Laws may be imperfect and enforcement may be difficult and spotty, but that's better than nothing. I'd rather have anti-bullying laws that protect kids 90% of the time and have difficulties 10% of the time, than have no laws to stop cyber bullying and leave kids vulnerable 100% of the time.
>
> Ben Leichtling, "Federal Laws Needed to Stop Cyber Bullying, Harassment and Abuse," Bullies Be Gone Blog, July 8, 2009. www.bulliesbegoneblog .com/2009/07/08/federal-anti-cyber-bullying-laws-needed- to-stop-harassment-bullying-and-abuse/.

---

1. Where two students killed twelve students and a teacher on April 20, 1999.

For example, you cannot falsely yell "FIRE" in a crowded theater. If you say it even once you can be held liable. Yet, you can repeatedly emotionally abuse someone with words, pictures, and false impressions online and get away scot-free.

The Megan Meier Cyberbullying Prevention Act would criminalize bullying like this when perpetrators hide behind the emboldening anonymity of the web. Severe online bullying must have consequences.

Current Supreme Court jurisprudence already recognizes some reasonable regulation of speech is consistent with the First Amendment. For example, the Court has found that true threats, commercial speech, slander, and

State Cyberbullying Laws

As of 2009, twenty states either had laws against cyberbullying or general anti-bullying laws that included protection from electronic harassment.

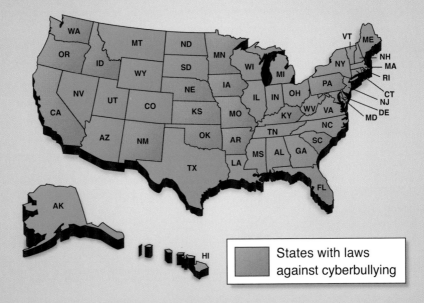

States with laws against cyberbullying

Taken from: *Bullying/Cyberbullying Prevention Law*, Anti-Defamation League, April 2009, pp. 9–10.

Some view cyberbullying as more abusive than face-to-face harassment because of the anonymity the Internet provides.

libel can be reasonably restricted consistent with the Constitution. Slander and libel law provide for different standards when the injured party is a public official or private person, and nothing in the Megan Meier Cyberbullying Prevention Act attempts to override that principle. Instead, the Act would give judges and juries discretion to recognize the difference between an annoying chain email, a righteously angry political blog post, or a miffed text to an ex-boyfriend and serious, repeated, hostile communications made with the intent to harm. I consulted with a variety of experts and law professors in crafting this bill to preserve our American freedom of speech *and* protect victims of cyberbullying.

Anti-Cyberbullying Laws Do Not Threaten Free Speech

Congress has no interest in censoring speech and it will not do so if it passes this bill. Put simply, this legislation would be used as a tool for a judge and jury to determine whether there is significant evidence to prove that a person "cyberbullied" another. That is: did they have the required intent, did they use electronic means of communication, and was the communication severe, hostile, and repeated. So—bloggers, emailers, texters, spiteful exes, and those who have blogged against this bill have no fear—your words are still protected under the same American values.

But the internet should not be the last refuge of scoundrels who use its anonymity to abuse, harass, and bully our children.

Analyze the essay:

1. Sanchez claims that anti-cyberbullying laws would not threaten free speech. Lisa Waananen, author of the following essay, disagrees. After reading both essays, with which author do you agree? Would laws against cyberbullying threaten free speech? Why or why not?

2. Sanchez is a congresswoman from California. She is also the primary author of the Megan Meier Cyberbullying Prevention Act which seeks to make cyberbullying illegal. Does knowing Sanchez's background and credentials make you more likely to agree with her argument? Why or why not?

Anti-Cyberbullying Policies Threaten Free Speech

Lisa Waananen

In the following essay Lisa Waananen warns that anti-cyberbullying policies could be used to curb free speech. She explains that oftentimes, cyberbullying is nothing more than people publishing unpopular or controversial comments and opinions. Even though some of these are mean or hurtful, such speech is protected by the First Amendment. Waananen warns that anti-cyberbullying policies could be used to censor all kinds of student publications, which are already vulnerable to scrutiny and censorship by school administrators. Furthermore, Waananen points out that many cyberbullying cases involve the protection of teachers and administrators from nasty speech, and adults need to be less sensitive to such comments. She concludes that laws against cyberbullying will end up being used to violate the free speech rights of America's students.

Waananen is a journalist and a graduate of the Edward R. Morrow School of Communication at Washington State University.

Consider the following questions:

1. Who is Katherine Evans and how does she factor into the author's argument?
2. Who, according to Professor Mary-Rose Papandrea, needs to have "thicker skin," and about what?
3. What happened at Tufts University in 2007, according to Waananen?

Lisa Waananen, "Weighing Fear Against Rights: Cyberbullying Hysteria Is Beating Up First Amendment Protections for Students," SPLC.org, Spring 2009. © 2009 Student Press Law Center. Reproduced by permission.

Katherine Evans was a frustrated high school student when she posted a rant about a teacher in November 2007 and invited others to "express your feelings of hatred." The three responding comments all supported the teacher instead, and Evans removed the message. But her writing still came to the school's attention—she was accused of violating the school's policy against cyberbullying and suspended for three days.

Parents and educators trying to crack down on "cyberbullying" tell painful stories about students harassing their classmates with text messages and posting hurtful rumors online—but as Evans found out, laws and policies against cyberbullying could open new routes to attack substantive student speech.

Free Speech Is Under Threat

In the first major case to appeal cyberbullying charges on First Amendment grounds, Evans is suing to get her disciplinary record cleared. Maria Kayanan, associate legal director at the American Civil Liberties Union of Florida, is working on the case. She said policies targeted at "mean girls and mean boys" are dangerous because they include conduct that happens away from school grounds.

"There's clearly a place for protecting children in schools from each other, because sometimes the bullying can pose imminent physical harm," Kayanan said. "But when you talk about the speech like [Evans's] or something that's published in a student newspaper critical of, say, the school administration or a teacher, under many schools' definitions of cyberbullying that would be prohibited. So it's a real smashup between the First Amendment and legitimate concerns, in some instances, to protect children."

People Need to Have "Thicker Skin"

Educators and legislators are tackling this new schoolyard menace with a flurry of policies that give administrators

Some believe that anti-cyberbullying policies could lead to violations of free speech rights.

control over students' electronic expression. In response to concern about the now-defunct JuicyCampus.com, the New Jersey attorney general told colleges and universities in the state to make sure their codes of conduct included the topic of "cyber-harassment."

Mary-Rose Papandrea, an assistant professor at the Boston College Law School, said the national focus on students' cyberbullying each other is a diversion from the actual First Amendment issues, because most cases so far involve a student who posted something offensive about a teacher or administrator.

"It's not really about protecting kids from other kids—and that could raise a whole host of other issues," she said. "When it is involving students who are poking fun at their teachers, the teachers and principals just need to have a thicker skin."

Anti-Cyberbullying Policies Could Be Used to Censor

Even policies created with good intentions like "promoting a safe environment" or "making all students comfortable" could open the door for censorship, said Will Creeley, director of legal and public advocacy for the Foundation for Individual Rights in Education.

It is not clear whether policies aimed at harassing e-mails and text messages could be used to censor online newspapers, students' blogs or comments from readers. One thing is for certain, Creeley said—some administrator somewhere will try.

"All of these understandable rationales for restricting speech, in the end, lead to abuse," he said.

Harassment policies—the low-tech older sibling of cyberbullying policies—have been used to justify censorship of students' opinions, Creeley said. At Tufts University in 2007, a conservative student paper was found guilty of violating the Bedford, Mass., school's harassment policy for satirical articles offensive to minority students. It would not be surprising to see cyberbullying policies used in the same way against online publications, Creeley said.

"Our concern about passing more legislation and much of the cyberbullying legislation we've seen is that it's broadly written, it's typically very vague, and it does threaten to swallow protected speech," he said.

We Must Protect Free Speech on the Internet

The First Amendment does not permit targeting speech merely because it is offensive, reprehensible, or even hurtful to the unsuspecting listener. . . . The solution to offensive online speech is not to engage in the knee-jerk reaction of saying it should be banned. . . . Ultimately, the only way for the Internet to remain a true marketplace of ideas for the 21st Century is to continue to promote the free exchange of information and speech, with the understanding that online speech can be as beneficial or as hurtful as speech occurring offline.

James Tucker, "Free Speech and 'Cyber-bullying,'" ACLU Blog of Rights, January 16, 2008. www.aclu .org/2008/01/16/free-speech-and-cyber-bullying.

The Fear That Lawful Speech Will Be Penalized

FIRE [Foundation for Individual Rights in Education] and the New Jersey chapter of the Society of Professional Journalists joined the Student Press Law Center in a letter of concern to New Jersey Attorney General Anne Milgram about the vagueness of her directive to the state's higher education institutions.

"An open-ended directive that colleges enact codes of conduct that punish the use of computers for 'bullying' will invariably cause some administrators to penalize lawful speech that falls within the protection of the First Amendment," the groups wrote in November 2008.

In contrast to traditional publications, administrators may be even more concerned about online speech because of its potentially global audience.

"A lot of the reasons schools are getting up in arms about the Internet speech are because they feel it reflects badly on the school," Papandrea said.

Avoid Getting Caught Up In the Cyberbullying Frenzy

The ramifications of this new medium are perplexing judges trying to apply old precedents to new kinds of speech, she said—and other people are conflicted about how they feel, too. Student newspapers that were read and promptly recycled in the past are now available to the whole world online, potentially forever.

"Before, if it's on the bathroom wall, you erase it. If it's in the kid's notebook, you throw it away. But this medium is different," said Clay Calvert, a professor and co-director of the Pennsylvania Center for the First Amendment at Pennsylvania State University. "And frankly the kids know the medium far better than many administrators do, and that's probably scary, too."

This underlying perception that technology makes unpleasant or offensive speech "worse" is part of what is troubling about this push to discipline cyberbullying, SPLC [Student Press Law Center] Director Frank LoMonte said. "The fact is that more people are likely to see graffiti on a bathroom stall at school than a student's blog entry, and as adults we ought not to be feeding the frenzy of vulnerable young people that, just because something is accessible electronically, it means 'the whole world' is reading it and believing it," LoMonte said. "Adults ought to be teaching kids exactly the opposite—that their value as people is not in any way defined by an anonymous insult on a social-networking page."

Analyze the essay:

1. In this essay, you read how Student Press Law Center director Frank LoMonte thinks that people are more likely to see nasty comments when they are graffitied on a bathroom stall at school versus written on a student's blog or social-networking page. Do you agree with LoMonte? Why or why not?

2. Waananen quotes from several sources to support the points she makes in her essay. Make a list of everyone she quotes, including their credentials and the nature of their comments. Then, analyze her sources— are they credible? Are they well qualified to speak on this subject? What specific points do they support?

Section Two:
Model Essays
and Writing
Exercises

The Five-Paragraph Essay

An *essay* is a short piece of writing that discusses or analyzes one topic. The five-paragraph essay is a form commonly used in school assignments and tests. Every five-paragraph essay begins with an *introduction*, ends with a *conclusion*, and features three *supporting paragraphs* in the middle.

The Thesis Statement. The introduction includes the essay's thesis statement. The thesis statement presents the argument or point the author is trying to make about the topic. The essays in this book all have different thesis statements because they are making different arguments about bullying.

The thesis statement should clearly tell the reader what the essay will be about. A focused thesis statement helps determine what will be in the essay; the subsequent paragraphs are spent developing and supporting its argument.

The Introduction. In addition to presenting the thesis statement, a well-written introductory paragraph captures the attention of the reader and explains why the topic being explored is important. It may provide the reader with background information on the subject matter or feature an anecdote that illustrates a point relevant to the topic. It could also present startling information that clarifies the point of the essay or put forth a contradictory position that the essay will refute. Further techniques for writing an introduction are found later in this section.

The Supporting Paragraphs. The introduction is then followed by three (or more) supporting paragraphs. These are the main body of the essay. Each paragraph presents and develops a *subtopic* that supports the essay's thesis statement. Each subtopic is spearhead-ed by a *topic sentence* and supported by its own facts, details, and examples. The writer can use various kinds of supporting material and details to back up the topic of each supporting paragraph. These may include statistics, quotations from people with special knowledge or exper-tise, historic facts, and anecdotes. A rule of good writing is that specific and concrete examples are more convinc-ing than vague, general, or unsupported assertions.

The Conclusion. The conclusion is the paragraph that closes the essay. Its function is to summarize or reiterate the main idea of the essay. It may recall an idea from the introduction or briefly examine the larger implica-tions of the thesis. Because the conclusion is also the last chance a writer has to make an impression on the reader, it is important that it not simply repeat what has been presented elsewhere in the essay but close it in a clear, final, and memorable way.

Although the order of the essay's component para-graphs is important, they do not have to be written in the order presented here. Some writers like to decide on a thesis and write the introduction paragraph first. Other writers like to focus first on the body of the essay, and write the introduction and conclusion later.

Pitfalls to Avoid

When writing essays about controversial issues such as bullying, it is important to remember that disputes over the material are common precisely because there are many different perspectives. Remember to state your arguments in careful and measured terms. Evaluate your topic fairly—avoid overstating negative qualities of one perspective or understating positive qualities of another. Use examples, facts, and details to support any asser-tions you make.

The Narrative Essay

Narrative writing is writing that tells a story or describes an event. Stories are something most people are familiar with since childhood. When you describe what you did on your summer vacation, you are telling a story. Journalists write stories of yesterday's events. Novelists write fictional stories about imagined events.

Stories are often found in essays meant to persuade. The previous section of this book provided you with examples of persuasive essays about bullying. These essays attempted to convince you to support specific arguments about bullying. In addition to making arguments, some of the authors of these essays also tell stories in which bullying plays a part. They used narrative writing to do this.

Components of Narrative Writing

All stories contain basic components *of character, setting,* and *plot*. These components answer four basic questions—who, when, where, and what—that readers need to make sense of the story being told.

Characters answer the question of whom the story is about. In a personal narrative using the first-person perspective ("My brother was bullied so badly he had to switch schools"), the characters are the writer and his brother. But writers can also tell the story of other people or characters ("To get back at her for stealing her boyfriend, Claire Howard forwarded racy pictures of her former friend Kelly to everyone in her address book") without being part of the story themselves.

The *setting* answers the questions of when and where the story takes place. The more details given about characters and setting, the more the reader learns about them and the author's views toward them. In Viewpoint One, author Sirdeaner Lynn Walker describes her house as the setting of the death of her son Carl. Model Essay Three describes the school the narrator attends. It is the setting for several instances of bullying.

The *plot* answers the question of what happens to the characters. It often involves conflict or obstacles that a story's character confronts and must somehow resolve. An example is found in Model Essay Three in this book, which tells the story of two girls who are bullied by a trio of popular girls. How the narrator chooses to act and how this affects the lives of the other characters affects the outcome of the story.

Some people distinguish narrative essays from stories in that narrative essays have a point—that is, in addition to telling a story, there is a general observation, argument, or insight that the author wants to impress upon the reader. In other words, narrative essays also answer "why" questions: Why did these particular events happen to the character? Why is this story worth retelling? What can be learned from this story? Why is it important? The story's point is the essay's thesis. For example, Viewpoint Six by Lisa Waananen uses the story of high school student Katherine Evans to argue that anti-cyberbullying policies are wrongly used to censor free speech.

Using Narrative Writing in Persuasive Essays

Narrative writing can be used in persuasive essays in several different ways. Stories can be used in the introductory paragraph(s) to grab the reader's attention and to introduce the thesis. Stories can compose all or part of the middle paragraphs that are used to support the thesis. They may even be used in concluding paragraphs as a way to restate and reinforce the essay's general point. Narrative essays may focus on one particular story, such as Viewpoint One, which focuses on the story of Carl Joseph Walker-Hoover. Or, like Model Essay One which spotlights the stories of Walker-Hoover, Ryan Halligan, and Jessica Logan, narrative essays may draw upon multiple stories to make their point.

A narrative story can also be used as one of several arguments or supporting points. Or, a narrative can take up an entire essay. Some stories are used as just one of several pieces of evidence that an author offers to make a point. In this type of essay, the author usually writes a formal conclusion that ties together for the reader the connection between the story and the point of the essay. In other narrative essays, the story discussed is so powerful that by the time the reader reaches the end of the narrative, the author's main point is clear, and they need not offer a formal conclusion.

In the following section, you will read some model essays on bullying that use narrative writing. You will also do exercises that will help you write your own narrative essays.

When Bullying Kills

Editor's Notes As you read in Preface B, narrative writing has several uses. In the real world, writers may incorporate the narrative technique into another type of essay, such as a persuasive or a cause-effect essay. They may also choose to use narrative only in portions of their essay. Instead of focusing their whole essay on a single story, they may use several different stories together.

This is the structure of the following model essay: it uses pieces of narration to discuss instances in which bullying has resulted in suicide. As you read, pay attention to the essay's components and how they are organized. Also note that all sources are cited using Modern Language Association (MLA) style.* For more information on how to cite your sources see Appendix C. In addition, consider the following:

1. How does the introduction engage the reader's attention?
2. How is narration used in the essay?
3. What purpose do the essay's quotes serve?
4. Would the essay be as effective if it contained only general arguments, and the stories of Carl Walker-Hoover, Ryan Halligan, and Jessica Logan had not been included?

Paragraph 1

The introductory paragraph lays out the topic to be discussed and expresses the author's argument, or thesis: that bullying results in suicide.

Bullying—sometimes regarded as a character-building rite of passage common to youth everywhere—must increasingly be viewed as a cruel, even criminal activity with deadly consequences. Indeed, too many young people have committed suicide after enduring cruel taunts and physical abuse from classmates and peers. Reading their stories is a heart-wrenching reminder of why bullying must be discouraged and young people must be kinder to each other.

Paragraph 2

April 6, 2009: this was the day Carl Joseph Walker-Hoover chose death as an escape from bullying. For much of his life, Carl was a happy, well-adjusted kid. He played football, basketball, and was a boy scout. He routinely volunteered to help the homeless and was active in his church. Yet he was relentlessly bullied at school and made fun of for the way he dressed and acted. His classmates called him "faggot" and "girlie," and frequently threatened him with violence. Just days before his suicide, while at school, he accidentally hit a television with his backpack, which careened into a girl, who yelled at him and threatened to hurt him. It is possible this incident was the final straw in a long line of bullying for Carl. At the age of eleven, he hung himself in his room with an extension cord while his mother cooked dinner downstairs. Said his mother, "What could make a child his age despair so much that he would take his own life? That question haunts me to this day." (Walker)

This is the topic sentence of Paragraph 2. It lets you know what the paragraph will focus on.

These specific details offer the reader a vivid picture of the bullying that Walker-Hoover endured.

Paragraph 3

On October 7, 2003, thirteen-year-old Ryan Halligan made the same decision as Carl. As his father was away on business and the rest of his family slept, Ryan hung himself in the bathroom in the early hours of the morning. His suicide came on the heels of a relentless bullying campaign from fellow students at his Vermont high school. Ryan suffered from a learning disorder that made him the butt of jokes at school; a girl he had a crush on also rejected him. Just prior to his death, Ryan shared a story about something embarrassing that happened to him while at the doctor with a supposed friend. The friend used the story to spread rumors that Ryan was gay. The bullying increased until finally Ryan was unable to take it any more. "For too long, we have let kids and adults bully others as a rite of passage into adulthood," said Ryan's father, John. "Nothing can ever bring back our Ryan. Nothing will ever heal our broken hearts." (Qtd. in "Ryan's Story")

This quote was taken from Viewpoint One. This book is filled with useful quotes, facts, statistics, and anecdotes that can be used in essays you write on bullying.

Paragraph 4

On July 3, 2008, another young life ended as a result of bullying. Eighteen-year-old Jessica Logan hung herself in her closet after being harassed about nude pictures she had texted to a former boyfriend. Logan's peers aggressively teased her, calling her "slut," "porn queen," and "whore." They made fun of her both in real life and online; there was no escape from the constant humiliation. "She was called filthy names, things thrown at her," said Jessica's mother, Cynthia. "Every single place she went they knew about that picture, they saw the picture. They knew about the picture! It's abuse. She was abused." (Qtd. in Paolello) Jessica could find no escape from the harassment. After attending the funeral of a friend who committed suicide, she came home and decided to do the same thing. She told her mother she loved her and went into her room, never to emerge alive again.

This quote from the victim's mother offers a compelling and first-person perspective on the matter. Get in the habit of filling your essays with compelling quotes from relevant sources.

What supporting details are offered in Paragraph 4?

Paragraph 5

Carl, Ryan, and Jessica are just a few of the bright, promising young people whose lives were cut short as a result of bullying. The world will never know what they might have become had they lived; their loved ones are forever robbed of their presence. Their families now work to raise awareness and pass anti-bullying legislation, but their lives will never be the same.

Works Cited

Walker, Sirdeaner Lynn. Testimony before the Subcommittee on Healthy Families and Communities and Subcommittee on Early Childhood, Elementary and Secondary Education of the House Education and Labor Committee. 8 Jul. 2009.

"Ryan's Story." < http://www.ryanpatrickhalligan.org/ > .

Paolello, Sheree. "Mom Loses Daughter over 'Sexting,' Demands Accountability." WLWT Cincinnati News.com. 9 Mar. 2009. < http://www.wlwt.com/news/18866515/detail.html > .

Exercise 1A: Create an Outline from an Existing Essay

It often helps to create an outline of the five-paragraph essay before you write it. The outline can help you organize the information, arguments, and evidence you have gathered during your research.

For this exercise, create an outline that could have been used to write Model Essay One: "When Bullying Kills." This "reverse engineering" exercise is meant to help familiarize you with how outlines can help classify and arrange information.

To do this you will need to

1. articulate the essay's thesis,
2. pinpoint important pieces of evidence,
3. flag quotes that supported the essay's idea, and
4. identify key points that supported the argument.

Part of the outline has already been started to give you an idea of the assignment.

Outline

I. Paragraph 1
Write the essay's thesis: Bullying can result in teen suicide.

II. Paragraph 2
Topic: The suicide of Carl Joseph Walker-Hoover
   Supporting Detail i.

   Supporting Detail ii.

III. Paragraph 3
Topic: The suicide of Ryan Halligan
   Supporting Detail i.

Supporting Detail ii. Quote from Ryan's father, John, expressing his feelings about his son's suicide.

IV. Paragraph 4
Topic:

Supporting Detail i.

Supporting Detail i.

V. Paragraph 5
Write the essay's conclusion:

Exercise 1B: Create an Outline for Your Own Essay

The first model essay expresses a particular point of view about bullying. For this exercise, your assignment is to find supporting ideas, choose specific and concrete details, create an outline, and ultimately write a five-paragraph essay making a different, even opposing, point about bullying. Your goal is to use narrative techniques to convince your reader.

Part I: Write a thesis statement.

The following thesis statement would be appropriate for an opposing narrative essay on bullying:

Only in very extreme cases does bullying result in suicide—usually there are other underlying issues, such as depression or mental illness, that contribute to the suicide.

Or, see the sample paper topics suggested in Appendix D for more ideas.

Part II: Brainstorm pieces of supporting evidence

Using information found in this book and from your own research, write down three arguments or pieces of evidence that support the thesis statement you selected. Then, for each of these three arguments, write down supportive facts, examples, and details that support it. These could be:

- statistical information
- personal memories and anecdotes
- quotes from experts, peers, or family members
- observations of people's actions and behaviors
- specific and concrete details

Supporting pieces of evidence for the above sample thesis statement might include:

- Quote from Larry Magid in Viewpoint Four of this book: "In the few known cases of suicide after cyberbullying, there are other contributing factors. . . . Cyberbullying is often accompanied by a pattern of offline bullying and sometimes there are other issues including long-term depression, problems at home, and self-esteem issues."
- Ryan Halligan, who committed suicide on October 7, 2003, suffered from depression in addition to enduring bullying at school.
- Points made by reporter Helen A.S. Popkin in "Cyberbullying Laws Won't Save Your Children," MSNBC.com, May 15, 2009. http://today.msnbc.msn.com/id/30751310/ns/technology_and_science_tech_and_gadgets/. Popkin contends that Megan Meier—who killed herself on October 17, 2006—had suicidal aspirations prior to being bullied online. Popkin also points out that Jessica Logan killed herself after attending the funeral of a friend who had committed suicide, "which increases suicide risk significantly."

Part III: Place the information from Part I in outline form.

Part IV: Write the arguments or supporting statements in paragraph form.

By now you have three arguments that support the essay's thesis statement, as well as supporting material. Use the outline to write out your three supporting arguments in paragraph form. Make sure each paragraph has a topic sentence that states the paragraph's thesis clearly and broadly. Then, add supporting sentences that express the facts, quotes, details, and examples that support the paragraph's argument. The paragraph may also have a concluding or summary sentence.

Death by MySpace

Editor's Notes The following piece of writing is another persuasive essay that uses narrative techniques to make its point. It tells the story of Megan Meier, a thirteen-year-old Missouri girl who committed suicide after being bullied online. The characters, setting, and plot are recounted in more detail than they would be in a simple anecdote in order to better engage the reader in the story. In this way the author relies on the power of the story itself to make the essay's point that cyberbullying is a serious problem that has deadly consequences.

The notes in the margins provide questions that will help you analyze how this essay is organized and written.

■ Refers to thesis and topic sentences

■ Refers to supporting details

Paragraph 1

He was everything she'd ever dreamed of—slightly older, into music, and seriously cute. Best of all, he liked her and thought she was pretty. MySpace had brought them together, and thirteen-year-old Megan Meier was happier than she'd been in months. But within a short period of time, Megan would be dead and the danger of Internet bullying would be tragically clear.

Because this essay tells a story, it doesn't have a formal thesis statement. Still, the main idea of the essay is expressed here and lets the reader know where the author is headed.

Paragraph 2

When sixteen-year-old Josh Evans asked to befriend Megan on the popular social networking site, she was thrilled. He sounded so cool—he said he played drums and guitar, and he owned a pet snake—and Megan thought he was hot. She wanted to talk on the phone, but Josh said he was new to her town of O'Fallon, Missouri, and told Megan he did not yet have a phone number. He claimed to be home schooled, which explained why no one else she was friends with knew him. The more the two e-mailed, the more she developed a crush. Megan was slightly overweight and suffered from attention deficit

Paragraph 2 develops the story's characters. What kinds of details do you learn about them?

69

disorder and depression, and her relationship with Josh made her feel, for the first time in a long time, happy and attractive. "Megan had a lifelong struggle with weight and self-esteem," said her mother, Tina. "And now she finally had a boy who she thought really thought she was pretty." (Qtd. in Pokin)

What point does this quote directly support?

Paragraph 3

But on October 15, 2006, Josh and Megan got into an argument. "I don't know if I want to be friends with you anymore because I've heard that you are not very nice to your friends," wrote Josh. (Qtd. in Pokin) Megan was surprised and confused, and the two began to fight. After exchanging a barrage of insults, Josh wrote, "You are a bad person and everybody hates you. . . . The world would be a better place without you." (Qtd. in Pokin) He forwarded her comments to other MySpace users, and within minutes, hundreds of people joined the assault, calling Megan a slut and other hurtful names, like "whore" and "fat ass." "Mom, they're being horrible!" cried Megan. (Qtd. in Maag) After an hour, she could take it no more. She ran sobbing into her room, where she hung herself in her closet with a belt. It was just weeks before her fourteenth birthday.

Note how the quotes in Paragraph 3 offer you a window into the characters' thoughts and actions.

Paragraph 4

Six weeks after Megan's death, it was revealed that Josh Evans did not exist. He had been created by a 47-year-old woman named Lori Drew, whose daughter Sarah was a former friend of Megan's. Megan and Sarah had had a falling out earlier in the year, and Drew wanted to get back at Megan for the way she had treated her daughter. So she created the fake MySpace account. Drew admitted she wanted to trick Megan and embarrass her online. Though she did not intend for the hoax to end in the girl's death, her actions—along with the anonymous, pile-on nature of the Internet—resulted in the tragic, needless death of a young girl desperate for acceptance.

How does this paragraph serve to advance the story's plot?

Paragraph 5

Megan is one of many teens who have committed suicide after experiencing online bullying. But her case is particularly upsetting because an adult was responsible for initiating the harassment. To the disappointment of Megan's family—and of supporters all around the country—Drew was eventually acquitted of wrongdoing in Megan's death and found guilty only of computer fraud. That she will not serve prison time for her role in Megan's death is difficult to accept by those seeking justice. Megan's death is a powerful lesson in just how dangerous bullying has become in the modern age.

Note how the conclusion returns to ideas discussed in the beginning of the essay.

Works Cited

Maag, Christopher. "A Hoax Turned Fatal Draws Anger but No Charges." *New York Times* 28 Nov 2007. < http://www .nytimes.com/2007/11/28/us/28hoax.html > .

Pokin, Steve. "A Real Person, a Real Death." *St. Charles Journal* 10 Nov 2007. < http://stcharlesjournal.stltoday .com/articles/2007/11/10/news/sj2tn20071110-1111 stc_pokin_l.ii1.txt > .

Exercise 2A: Identifying and Organizing Components of the Narrative Essay

As you read in Preface B of this section, narrative essays contain certain elements, including *characters*, *setting*, and *plot*. This exercise will help you identify these elements and place them in an organized structure of paragraphs.

For this exercise you will isolate and identify the components of a narrative essay. Model Essay Three, *Confessions of a Former Bully*, is a good source to practice on. You may also, if you choose, use experiences from your own life or that of your friends and family. Part of the exercise is filled out for you using the narrative elements from "Death by MySpace."

Part A: Isolate and write down story elements

Setting

The setting of a story is the time and place the story happens. Such information helps orient the reader. Does the story take place in the distant or recent past? Does it take place in a typical American community or exotic locale?

Model Essay Two	"Confessions of a Former Bully"	Other Story
O'Fallon, Missouri Megan Meier's house October 2006		

Characters

Who is the story about? If there is more than one character, how are they related? At what stage of life are they? What are their aspirations and hopes? What makes them distinctive and interesting to the reader?

Model Essay Two	"Confessions of a Former Bully"	Other Story
Megan Meier, 13 "Josh Evans," 16 Lori Drew, 47		

Pivotal Event

Most stories contain at least one single, discrete event on which the narrative hinges. It can be a turning point that changes lives or a specific time when a character confronts a challenge, comes to a flash of understanding, or resolves a conflict.

Model Essay Two	"Confessions of a Former Bully"	Other Story
Megan hangs herself in her closet.		

Events/Actions Leading up to the Pivotal Event

What are the events that happen to the characters? What are the actions the characters take? These elements are usually told in chronological order in a way that advances the action—that is, each event proceeds naturally and logically from the preceding one.

Model Essay Two	"Confessions of a Former Bully"	Other Story
Megan is befriended online by "Josh Evans," who gains Megan's trust and becomes the object of her affection. Evans suddenly turns on Megan and initiates a rash of online bullying that results in the girl's suicide.		

Events/Actions That Stem from Pivotal Event

What events/actions are the results of the pivotal event in the story? How were the lives of the characters of the stories changed?

Model Essay Two	"Confessions of a Former Bully"	Other Story
After Megan's suicide, it is revealed that Evans was not a real person, but one created by Lori Drew. Drew is found guilty of computer fraud.		

Point/Moral

What is the reason for telling the story? Stories generally have a lesson or purpose that is ultimately clear to the reader, whether the point is made explicitly or implied. Stories could serve as specific examples of a general social problem. They could be teaching tools describing behavior and actions that the reader should either avoid or emulate.

Model Essay Two	"Confessions of a Former Bully"	Other Story
Story is a tragic example of the serious consequences of cyberbullying.		

Part B: Writing down narrative elements in paragraph form

Since stories vary greatly, there are many ways to approach telling them. One possible way of organizing the story elements you have structured is as follows:

Paragraph 1: Tell the reader the setting of the story and introduce the characters. Provide descriptive details of both.

Paragraph 2: Introduce the plot—what happens in the story. Tell the events in chronological order, with each event advancing the action.

Paragraph 3: Describe the pivotal event in detail, and its immediate aftermath.

Paragraph 4: Tell the short-term and/or long-term ramifications of the pivotal event. This paragraph could also include the point or moral of the story.

Paragraph 5: Conclude the story in a memorable and interesting way.

Exercise 2B: Examining Introductions and Conclusions

Most essays feature introductory and concluding paragraphs that are used to frame the main ideas being presented. Along with presenting the essay's thesis statement, well-written introductions should grab the attention of the reader and make clear why the topic being explored is important. The conclusion reiterates the essay's thesis and is also the last chance for the writer to make an impression on the reader. Strong introductions and conclusions can greatly enhance an essay's effect on an audience.

The Introduction

There are several techniques that can be used to craft an introductory paragraph. An essay can start with:

- an anecdote: a brief story that illustrates a point relevant to the topic.
- startling information: facts or statistics that elucidate the point of the essay.
- setting up and knocking down a position: a position or claim believed by proponents of one side of a controversy, followed by statements that challenge that claim.

- historical perspective: an example of the way things used to be that leads into a discussion of how or why things work differently now.
- summary information: general introductory information about the topic that feeds into the essay's thesis statement.

Problem One

Reread the introductory paragraphs of the model essays and of the viewpoints in Section One. Identify which of the techniques described above are used in the example essays. How do they grab the attention of the reader? Are their thesis statements clearly presented?

The Conclusion

The conclusion brings the essay to a close by summarizing or returning to its main ideas. Good conclusions, however, go beyond simply repeating these ideas. Strong conclusions explore a topic's broader implications and reiterate why it is important to consider. They may frame the essay by returning to an anecdote featured in the opening paragraph. Or, they may close with a quotation or refer back to an event in the essay. In opinionated essays, the conclusion can reiterate which side the essay is taking or ask the reader to reconsider a previously held position on the subject.

Problem Two

Reread the concluding paragraphs of the model essays and of the viewpoints in Section One. Which were most effective in driving their arguments home to the reader? What sorts of techniques did they use to do this? Did they appeal emotionally to the reader, or bookend an idea or event referenced elsewhere in the essay?

Confessions of a Former Bully

Editor's Notes Essays drawn from memories or personal experiences are called personal narratives. The following essay is this type of narrative. It is not based on research or the retelling of someone else's experiences, such as the other narrative essays you have read in this book. Instead, this essay consists of an autobiographical story that recounts memories of an event that happened to the writer.

The essay differs from the first two model essays in that it is written from the subjective, or first-person ("I"), point of view. It is important that you learn to master the personal narrative, as it is this type of essay that is frequently required by college, university, and other academic admissions boards. Personal narratives also tend to be required of candidates seeking to win scholarships and other contests.

The essay is also different from the previous model essays in that it has more than five paragraphs. Many ideas require more than five paragraphs in order to be adequately developed. Moreover, the ability to write a sustained essay is a valuable skill. Learning how to develop a longer piece of writing gives you the tools you will need to advance academically.

Refers to thesis and topic sentences

Refers to supporting details

Paragraph 1

Every school has a Jackie Meeter. You know, the kind of outcast that *everyone* can agree to hate. The popular kids particularly tortured Jackie. In gym class they'd throw dodge balls hard at her, leaving her covered with bright red welts. She was always picked last for teams and projects. It must have been humiliating for her to stand there in front of everyone, watching people pair off, knowing the teacher would eventually force her to partner with someone against their will. At lunch she sat all by herself at a table in the corner. Sometimes she would be absent

Because this is a personal narrative it does not have a thesis statement like a more formal essay would have. However, the main topic of the essay is still discussed upfront.

from the cafeteria entirely; these were the days she ate alone in the girls' bathroom in the school basement.

Paragraph 2

It's hard to say why everyone hated Jackie so much. She just kind of rubbed people the wrong way. She was overweight but always wore slightly revealing clothes that were too tight. This made her an easy target of the fashion-conscious students. She also liked music by bands no one else had ever heard of, and weird, old movies. She was a bit of a show-off, and even, at times, a liar; more than once she was caught bragging about ski trips and vacations to Europe, but no one actually believed she had ever been anywhere farther than a few hours from our small suburban town. But she was no more flawed than any other person at our school—it was just like the universe had singled her out to bear the brunt of social abuse.

Paragraph 3

Neither popular nor a total outcast, I existed in a social purgatory, an in-between world in which surviving socially meant knowing who to befriend and who to avoid. Jackie was definitely the kind of person to avoid, and this is why my friendship with her took place in secret, where no one else could learn of its existence. In private, we hung out, and we had a lot of fun. She lived around the corner from me and we had been friends since we were little. We rode bikes around our neighborhood and played in the stream down the street from our houses. In the privacy of her backyard tree house we shared secrets about boys we liked and girls we hated. As she sunk lower on the social totem pole at school, I distanced myself from her in public, yet continued to be her friend in private. I knew it was wrong and two-faced of me, but it seemed like social suicide to do otherwise. Poor Jackie was so desperate for company, she agreed to pretend we weren't friends when we were at school.

A person's internal thoughts can help reveal character and advance the plot—what the character decides to do and why.

What have you learned about the characters? What motivates them? What kind of people are they?

Paragraph 4

One day some of the popular kids confronted me about my friendship with Jackie, and forced me to make a choice. Elissa Bookbinder, flanked by her two best friends, Eva Danziger and Samantha Welsh, approached me in the school library. The three of them were beyond popular—at my school, they constituted teen royalty.

Paragraph 5

"So, Eva saw you hanging out with Meeter down by Grover Park last weekend," said Elissa, tossing her long, blonde hair over one shoulder. "Didn't realize you were into losers."

Paragraph 6

"Oh, we weren't hanging out," I said quickly. "I just ran into her and she like, started talking to me and I was like, ugh, whatever, stop talking to me right now."

"Is that a fact?" said Elissa.

"Uh, yeah. I *really* don't like that girl." I didn't sound very convincing.

Elissa looked over her shoulder at Eva and Samantha. "Prove it," she said. Both girls nodded.

Does the dialogue sound natural to you? What details or features enhance it?

Paragraph 7

"How am I supposed to do that?" I asked. "Besides, I don't have to prove anything to you."

Elissa put her face really close to mine. I could smell the honey lavender body spritz with which she was always freshening herself.

"You'll prove it," she said, "or you'll pay."

Just then the bell rang, signifying the end of the period. I rolled my eyes at Elissa and went to class, hoping I had escaped her wrath.

Paragraph 8

But over the next week, the three girls made my life a living hell. On Monday I found a dissected worm in my locker; on Tuesday, they taped a rotten sandwich to the underside of my desk. On Wednesday more than 30 prank calls were made to my home phone—some came as late as 1 A.M., which made my parents furious. On Thursday, Elissa had two members of the football team follow me around the hallways. Wherever I went they tried to block my path, trip me, or knock books out of my arms. By Friday I couldn't take it anymore. I found Elissa behind the auditorium, where she hung out with her cronies.

How does this paragraph serve to move the plot forward?

Paragraph 9

"Look, this last week has been really annoying, obviously, so whatever—how do you want me to prove that I hate Jackie Meeter as much as you do?"

Elissa smiled a satisfied, snide grin. "Rumor has it you live near Meeter's house. Think you can gain access?"

Paragraph 10

The plan was simple. I was to invite myself over to Jackie's house under the pretense of borrowing one of her lame old movies. While there, I was supposed to steal something personal—a bra, an embarrassing photo, that sort of thing—that Elissa could use to humiliate her.

Paragraph 11

Wanting to get the whole escapade over with, I went to Jackie's house right after school. She was excited to have me over. Her enthusiasm made me feel even more guilty.

Paragraph 12

"You are just going to love these Bob Hope movies," she said. "You know, very few people realize how groundbreaking they were. And so funny! You'll love them. Seriously."

"Yeah I can't wait to uh, watch them, and stuff," I said. I was distracted, too busy searching Jackie's room for something Elissa might want.

Paragraph 13

"Here's *Road to Morocco* and *Fancy Pants*." She threw the movies on my lap in an excited rush. "I also have *Son *of Paleface* somewhere around here . . . let me check my brother's room. It's just the funniest when Jane Russell gives Bob Hope sleeping pills!"

Paragraph 14

She walked across the hall and I knew I had to grab something fast. My eye fell upon a beaten up composition book on the ground. Her journal! Sure, journals are private, I thought, but that's better than her bra or something super embarrassing that can be run up the school's flagpole, right? I stuffed it in my backpack just as Jackie came back with the movie.

Are you interested in the characters and their motivations? Do they seem like real people to you? Personal narratives should strive for a realistic, natural tone.

Paragraph 15

"I found it! Here you go. Oh man, there's this one scene—"

   "Uh thanks, yeah, I'll watch it this weekend," I snatched it from her and before she could say anything else, ran out the door.

Paragraph 16

The next day I dutifully turned the journal over to Elissa. I didn't even read it first. I just wanted to be done with this dirty business. Elissa, however, read every word—*and* photocopied it and distributed it to the whole school. She had each copy bound and printed with a cover that read, "Jackie Meeter's Sick Twisted Thoughts." All of Jackie's most private musings and deepest secrets were on mortifying display. She had written about how she had lied to everyone about going skiing in the Alps; she had written that she had a third nipple. She had written that she had kissed her cousin at a family gathering the previous summer; she had written about how she often snuck into her kitchen at 2 A.M. and ate leftovers with her fingers. Most private, she had written about how she thought she was probably a lesbian, and kept a list of girls in school she thought were lesbians, too.

Paragraph 17

After the journal was printed, Jackie's life was essentially over. She couldn't go anywhere without being mocked and harassed. Everyone knew her most private thoughts and embarrassing moments, and she was now forced to live them, over and over, in front of the whole world. People took the cruelty to a whole new level. They screamed, "Make way for the Third Nipple!" when she walked down the hall. Someone graffitied her car, tagging "Dyke Nipple Queen" in bright orange spray paint. She started to get anonymous phone calls from people threatening to hurt her. Eventually she couldn't take it anymore. Her parents pulled her out of our school and her whole family moved out of town.

Paragraph 18

Personal narratives are not expected to have a formal conclusion like other essays, but they must still tie the story's ideas to a close.

Although I never saw Jackie Meeter again, I'll never forget her—or forgive myself for playing a part in the cruel bullying campaign that snowballed against her. Stealing her journal and denying our friendship didn't make me any more popular—it only made me deeply ashamed of myself.

Exercise 3A: Practice Writing a Scene with Dialogue

The previous model essay used scene and dialogue to make a point. For this exercise, you will practice creative writing techniques to draft a one- or two-paragraph scene with dialogue. First, take another look at Model Essay Three and examine how dialogue is used.

When writing dialogue, it is important to:

1. Use natural-sounding language.
2. Include a few details showing character gestures and expressions as they speak.
3. Avoid overuse of speaker tags with modifiers, such as "he said stupidly," "she muttered softly," "I shouted angrily," and so on.
4. Indent and create a new paragraph when speakers change.
5. Place quotation marks at the beginning and end of a character's speech.

Scene-Writing Practice

Interview a classmate, friend, or family member. Focus on a specific question about bullying, such as:

- Have you ever known anyone who has been bullied or bullied someone else? If so, what was the situation? Who was involved? Where did it take place? What did they do about it?
- What would you do if you ever witnessed an act of bullying? How would you feel? What might you say?
- Why do you think people bully others?

Take notes while you interview your subject. Write down what he or she says as well as any details that are provided. Ask probing questions that reveal how the subject felt, what they said, and how they acted. Make sure to establish a location for your scene, and include realistic descriptions of the place where the action occurred. Finally, use your notes and ideas to create a brief scene with dialogue.

But I Can't Write That

One aspect of personal narrative writing is that you are revealing to the reader something about yourself. Many people enjoy this part of writing, but others have trouble sharing their personal stories—especially if they reveal something embarrassing or something that could be used to get them in trouble. In these cases, what are your options?

- ✔ Talk with your teacher about your concerns. Will this narrative be shared in class? Can the teacher pledge confidentiality?
- ✔ Change the story from being about yourself to a story about a friend. This will involve writing in the third person rather than the first person.
- ✔ Change a few identifying details and names to disguise characters and settings.
- ✔ Pick a different topic or thesis that you do not mind sharing.

Exercise: Write Your Own Narrative Five-Paragraph Essay

Using the information from this book, write your own five-paragraph narrative essay that deals with bullying. You can use the resources in this book for information about bullying and how to structure a narrative essay.

The following steps are suggestions on how to get started.

Step One: Choose your topic.
The first step is to decide what topic to write your narrative essay on. Is there any subject that particularly fascinates you? Is there an issue you strongly support or strongly oppose? Is there a topic you feel personally connected to or have personal experience dealing with? Ask yourself such questions before selecting your essay topic. Refer to Appendix D: Sample Essay Topics if you need help selecting a topic.

Step Two: Write down questions and answers about the topic.
Before you begin writing, you will need to think carefully about what ideas your essay will contain. This is a process known as *brainstorming*. Brainstorming involves asking yourself questions and coming up with ideas to discuss in your essay. Possible questions that will help you with the brainstorming process include:

- Why is this topic important?
- Why should people be interested in this topic?
- How can I make this essay interesting to the reader?
- What question am I going to address in this paragraph or essay?
- What facts, ideas, or quotes can I use to support the answer to my question?

Questions especially for narrative essays include:

- Have I chosen a compelling story to examine?
- Does the story support my thesis statement?

- What qualities do my characters have? Are they interesting?
- Does my narrative essay have a clear beginning, middle, and end?
- Does my essay evoke a particular emotion or response from the reader?

Step Three: Gather facts, ideas, and anecdotes related to your topic.

This book contains several places to find information, including the viewpoints and the appendices. In addition, you may want to research the books, articles, and Web sites listed in Section Three, or do additional research in your local library. You can also conduct interviews if you know someone who has a compelling story that would fit well in your essay.

Step Four: Develop a workable thesis statement.

Use what you have written down in steps two and three to help you articulate the main point or argument you want to make in your essay. It should be expressed in a clear sentence and make an arguable or supportable point.

Example:

Anti-bullying legislation threatens students' free speech.

> This could be the thesis statement of a narrative essay that includes stories of how students' free speech rights have been infringed upon by anti-bullying legislation.

Step Five: Write an outline or diagram.

1. Write the thesis statement at the top of the outline.
2. Write roman numerals I, II, and III on the left side of the page with A, B, and C under each numeral.
3. Next to each roman numeral, write down the best ideas you came up with in step three. These should all directly relate to and support the thesis statement.
4. Next to each letter write down information that supports that particular idea.

Step Six: Write the three supporting paragraphs.
Use your outline to write the three supporting paragraphs. Write down the main idea of each paragraph in sentence form. Do the same thing for the supporting points of information. Each sentence should support the paragraph of the topic. Be sure you have relevant and interesting details, facts, and quotes. Use transitions when you move from idea to idea to keep the text fluid and smooth. Sometimes, although not always, paragraphs can include a concluding or summary sentence that restates the paragraph's argument.

Step Seven: Write the introduction and conclusion.
See Exercise 2B for information on writing introductions and conclusions.

Step Eight: Read and rewrite.
As you read, check your essay for the following:

- ✔ Does the essay maintain a consistent tone?
- ✔ Do all paragraphs reinforce your general thesis?
- ✔ Do all paragraphs flow from one to the other? Do you need to add transition words or phrases?
- ✔ Have you quoted from reliable, authoritative, and interesting sources?
- ✔ Is there a sense of progression throughout the essay?
- ✔ Does the essay get bogged down in too much detail or irrelevant material?
- ✔ Does your introduction grab the reader's attention?
- ✔ Does your conclusion reflect back on any previously discussed material, or give the essay a sense of closure?
- ✔ Are there any spelling or grammatical errors?

**Section Three:
Supporting
Research
Material**

Facts About Bullying

Editor's Note: These facts can be used in reports to reinforce or add credibility when making important points or claims.

Bullying has three key factors:
- The behavior is aggressive and intended to cause harm or distress; it is not accidental.
- The behavior is repeated over time.
- The behavior involves a power imbalance; that is, a more powerful bully torments a weaker or more vulnerable target.

Cyberbullying differs from traditional bullying in three important ways:
- It can occur at any time, day or night.
- It can be anonymous, and therefore difficult and sometimes impossible to trace.
- The anonymity and physical remove of the Internet makes it possible for a weaker, more vulnerable person to bully a more powerful target online.

According to *Indicators of School Crime and Safety: 2009*, by the National Center for Education Statistics:
- 32 percent of students aged twelve to eighteen report being involved in bullying as a bully, a target of bullying, or both;
- 21 percent of students experienced bullying consisting of being made fun of;
- 18 reported being the target of rumors;
- 11 percent reported being pushed, shoved, tripped, or spat on;
- 6 percent said they were threatened with physical harm;
- 5 percent said they were excluded from activities on purpose;

- 4 percent reported they were pressured to do things they did not want to do or their property was destroyed on purpose.

According to the Council on Scientific Affairs of the American Medical Association:
- Physical bullying (hitting, kicking, shoving, spitting) increases in elementary school, peaks in middle school, and decreases in high school.
- Verbal bullying (taunting, racial slurs, obscene gestures, gossip and rumors, being excluded) remains constant through high school.

According to a 2009 Bureau of Justice Statistics study:
- 34 percent of white students report being bullied at school
- 27 percent of Hispanic students report being bullied at school
- 18 percent of Asian students report being bullied at school

According to the Health Resources and Services Administration:
- Bullying often goes unreported, either because child and adolescent victims fear retaliation from bullies, or because victims fear adults will not take their complaint seriously or will embarrass them by reacting inappropriately.
- Young people who bully are more likely than those who do not bully to get into fights, vandalize property, skip school, drop out of school, smoke, and drink alcohol.
- The most common method of cyberbullying is through instant messaging, followed by chat rooms, e-mails, and messages posted on social networking sites.
- 45 percent of preteens and 30 percent of teens who are cyberbullied received the messages while at school.

- 44 percent of preteens and 70 percent of teens who are cyberbullied received the messages at home.

According to Stop Bullying Now.com, common reasons for bullying include:
- uncontrolled anger
- revenge
- jealousy
- violence in everyday surroundings
- death or illness of a loved one
- family financial hardships
- parental substance abuse
- learning disabilities
- need for attention
- entertainment/boredom
- lack of social skills

According to a study by Norwegian bullying researcher Dan Olweus:
- Low self-esteem is *not* a common trait of bullies. Contrary to popular belief, kids who bully generally feel good about themselves and even have high self-regard.
- There is a strong connection between school-age bullying of other students and legal and criminal problems as an adult: 60 percent of study subjects identified as bullies in grades six to nine had at least one criminal conviction by age twenty-four.
- 40 percent had three or more convictions.

Bullying situations usually involve bystanders as well as a bully and a target. PBS Kids reports several reasons why bystanders let bullying occur:
- The bully is someone others look up to or want to hang out with.
- Siding with the bully makes bystanders feel strong.
- They are entertained by the bullying.
- They think protesting will not help.

- They're afraid of being turned on by the bully for speaking out.
- Watching the bullying is a way to release their own frustrations and aggression without actually hurting anyone.

A 2008 Yale School of Medicine study reported a link between being bullied and thoughts of suicide in children. In five studies reviewed by Yale researchers, not only the children being bullied but also the children who were the bullies were two to nine times more likely to report suicidal thoughts than other children were.

A 2009 U.S. Department of Health and Human Services report found the following about gender and bullying:
- Boys bully more than girls do, but girls are slightly more likely than boys to report being bullied at school; twice as many girls than boys report being cyberbullied during the school year.
- Boys report being bullied by boys; girls report being bullied by both girls and boys.
- Boys are more likely to be perpetrators or targets of physical bullying. Girls are more likely to be perpetrators or targets of rumor-spreading, sexual insults, and social exclusion.

According to the Bureau of Justice Statistics in 2009, of all students who reported being bullied during the school year:
- 79 percent said they were bullied inside the school
- 23 percent said they were bullied outside on school grounds
- 8 percent said they were bullied on the school bus
- 63 percent said they were bullied once or twice during the year
- 7 percent reported being bullied almost daily

Children and adolescents who are bullies, the targets of bullies, or both are three to five times more likely than non-bullied individuals to have headaches, insomnia, abdominal pain, persistent colds and cough, anxiety, and depression, according to the federal Stop Bullying Now! campaign.

The U.S. Secret Service and the Department of Education studied thirty-seven incidents of targeted school violence, including school shootings, between 1974 and 2000. According to their *Safe School Initiative Report*, three-fourths of attackers felt persecuted and bullied prior to the attack.

A 2008 study by the Swedish National Council for Crime Prevention reviewed fifty-nine anti-bullying programs and found the following:
- Schools with anti-bullying programs had 17 to 23 percent fewer incidents of bullying and victimization than schools without anti-bullying programs.
- The most important elements of an effective anti-bullying program were parent training, improved playground supervision, disciplinary methods, school conferences, classroom rules, videos, and group work for counselors, teachers, and administrators as well as students.
- The longer and more intense the program, the greater the decrease in victimization.

According to the U.S. Department of Health and Human Services, Health Resources and Services Administration, common bullying prevention and intervention strategies that are *not* effective include:
- zero tolerance (student exclusion)
- group treatment for children who bully
- simple, short-term solutions

Finding and Using Sources of Information

No matter what type of essay you are writing, it is necessary to find information to support your point of view. You can use sources such as books, magazine articles, newspaper articles, and online articles.

Using Books and Articles

You can find books and articles in a library by using the library's computer or cataloging system. If you are not sure how to use these resources, ask a librarian to help you. You can also use a computer to find many magazine articles and other articles written specifically for the Internet.

You are likely to find a lot more information than you can possibly use in your essay, so your first task is to narrow it down to what is likely to be most usable. Look at book and article titles. Look at book chapter titles, and examine the book's index to see if it contains information on the specific topic you want to write about. (For example, if you want to write about bullying and you find a book about child psychology, check the chapter titles and index to be sure it contains information related to bullying before you bother to check out the book.)

For a five—paragraph essay, you do not need a great deal of supporting information, so quickly try to narrow down your materials to a few good books and magazine or Internet articles. You do not need dozens. You might even find that one or two good books or articles contain all the information you need.

You probably do not have time to read an entire book, so find the chapters or sections that relate to your topic, and skim these. When you find useful information, copy it onto a note card or notebook. You should look for supporting facts, statistics, quotations, and examples.

Using the Internet

When you select your supporting information, it is important that you evaluate its source. This is especially important with information you find on the Internet. Because nearly anyone can put information on the Internet, there is as much bad information as good information. Before using Internet information—or any information—determine if the source seems to be reliable. Is the author or Internet site sponsored by a legitimate organization? Is it from a government source? Does the author have any special knowledge or training relating to the topic you are looking up? Does the article give any indication of where its information comes from?

Using Your Supporting Information

When you use supporting information from a book, article, interview or other source, there are three important things to remember:

1. *Make it clear whether you are using a direct quotation or a paraphrase.* If you copy information directly from your source, you are quoting it. You must put quotation marks around the information, and tell where the information comes from. If you put the information in your own words, you are paraphrasing it.

Here is an example of a using a quotation:

Law professor Jonathan Turley suggests that schools take more extreme measures to clamp down on bullying: "While many will chafe at the notion of moving from hall monitors to personal injury lawyers, litigation could succeed in forcing schools to take bullying more seriously."

Here is an example of a brief paraphrase of the same passage:

Law professor Jonathan Turley suggests that schools take more extreme measures to clamp down on bullying. He believes that schools should be encouraged to take bullying as seriously as possible, and that students who are guilty of bullying their peers should be able to be sued in court.

2. *Use the information fairly.* Be careful to use supporting information in the way the author intended it. For example, it is unfair to quote an author as saying, "We overreact to bullying," when he or she intended to say, "We overreact to bullying very rarely—in most cases, bullying is a serious and possibly life-threatening problem for children." This is called taking information out of context. This is using supporting evidence unfairly.

3. *Give credit where credit is due.* Giving credit is known as citing. You must use citations when you use someone else's information, but not every piece of supporting information needs a citation.

   • If the supporting information is general knowledge—that is, it can be found in many sources—you do not have to cite your source.
   • If you directly quote a source, you must cite it.
   • If you paraphrase information from a specific source, you must cite it.

If you do not use citations where you should, you are *plagiarizing*—or stealing—someone else's work.

Citing Your Sources

There are a number of ways to cite your sources. Your teacher will probably want you to do it in one of three ways:
   • Informal: As in the example in number 1 above, tell where you got the information as you present it in the text of your essay.
   • Informal list: At the end of your essay, place an unnumbered list of all the sources you used. This tells the reader where, in general, your information came from.

- Formal: Use numbered footnotes or endnotes. Footnotes or endnotes are generally placed at the end of an article or essay, although they may be placed elsewhere depending on your teacher's requirements.

Works Cited

Turley, Jonathan. "Bullying's Day In Court." *USA Today* 15 Jul. 2008. < http://blogs.usatoday.com/oped/2008/07/bullyings-day-i.html > .

Using MLA Style to Create a Works Cited List

You will probably need to create a list of works cited for your paper. These include materials that you quoted from, relied heavily on, or consulted to write your paper. There are several different ways to structure these references. The following examples are based on Modern Language Association (MLA) style, one of the major citation styles used by writers.

Book Entries

For most book entries you will need the author's name, the book's title, where it was published, what company published it, and the year it was published. This information is usually found on the inside of the book. Variations on book entries include the following:

A book by a single author:
> Friedman, Thomas. *Hot, Flat, and Crowded: Why We Need a Green Revolution—and How It Can Renew America*. New York: Farrar, Straus and Giroux, 2008.

Two or more books by the same author:
> Pollen, Michael. *The Omnivore's Dilemma: A Natural History of Four Meals*. New York: Penguin Books, 2006.
> ———. *Botany of Desire: A Plant's-Eye View of the World*. New York: Random House, 2002.

A book by two or more authors:
> Esposito, John L., and Dalia Mogahed. *Who Speaks For Islam? What a Billion Muslims Really Think*. Washington, D.C.: Gallup Press, 2008.

A book with an editor:
> Skancke, Jennifer S., ed. *Introducing Issues with Opposing Viewpoints: Stem Cell Research.* Detroit: Greenhaven, 2008.

Periodical and Newspaper Entries

Entries for sources found in periodicals and newspapers are cited a bit differently than books. For one, these sources usually have a title and a publication name. They also may have specific dates and page numbers. Unlike book entries, you do not need to list where newspapers or periodicals are published or what company publishes them.

An article from a periodical
> Aldhous, Peter. "China's Burning Ambition." *Nature.* Vol. 435 Iss. 7046 30 Jun 2005:1152–1155.

An unsigned article from a periodical:
> "Contraception in Middle School?" *Harvard Crimson* 21 Oct. 2007.

An article from a newspaper:
> Cunningham, Roseanna. "Care, Not Euthanasia, Is the Answer to the 'Problem' of the Elderly." *Sunday Times* (London) 20 Jul. 2008: 21.

Internet Sources

To document a source you found online, try to provide as much information as possible, including the author's name, the title of the document, date of publication or of last revision, the URL, and your date of access.

A Web source:
> Mieszkowski, Katharine. "Plastic Bags Are Killing Us." Salon.com. 10 Aug. 2007. < http://www.salon.com/news/feature/2007/08/10/plastic-bags/index.html >. Accessed September 9, 2008.

Your teacher will tell you exactly how information should be cited in your essay. Generally, the very least information needed is the original author's name and the name of the article or other publication.

Be sure you know exactly what information your teacher requires before you start looking for your supporting information so that you know what information to include with your notes.

Sample Essay Topics

Bullying Is a Learned Behavior
Bullying Is Genetically Caused
Violent Video Games Contribute to Bullying
Movies and Reality TV Encourage Young People to Bully
Sexting Contributes to Bullying

Physical Bullying Is More Harmful than Verbal Bullying
Verbal Bullying Is More Harmful than Physical Bullying
Bullying Causes Youths to Commit Suicide
Bullying Does Not Cause Youths to Commit Suicide
The Media Exaggerate the Link Between Bullying and Suicide

Bullying of Gay and Lesbian Youth Is a Serious Problem
School Gay-Straight Alliances Can Reduce Homophobic Bullying
Racial Bullying Is a Growing Problem

Facebook Should Censor Bullying Comments
Facebook Censorship of Bullying Comments Is a Violation of Privacy and Free Speech
Cyberbullying Is Impossible to Stop
Cyberbullying Is Easy to Stop

Anti-Bullying Programs Make Schools Safer
School Anti-Bullying Programs Are Ineffective
Zero-Tolerance Policies Decrease Bullying in Schools
Zero-Tolerance Policies Do Not Decrease Bullying in Schools

Bystanders Are Responsible for Stopping School Bullying

Parents Are Responsible for Stopping Student Bullying

Schools Are Responsible for Stopping Student Bullying

Schools Should Not Be Held Responsible for Student Cyberbullying

Children Have to Learn to Resolve Bullying on Their Own

Organizations to Contact

The editors have compiled the following list of organizations concerned with the issues debated in this book. The descriptions are derived from materials provided by the organizations. All have publications or information available for interested readers. The list was compiled on the date of publication of the present volume; the information provided here may change. Be aware that many organizations take several weeks or longer to respond to queries, so allow as much time as possible.

American Psychological Association (APA)
750 First St. NE, Washington, DC 20002-4242
phone: (800) 374-2721• e-mail: public.affairs@apa.org
Web site: www.apa.org

The 150,000-member APA is the primary scientific and professional psychology organization in the United States. Its official position is that bullying exerts short- and long-term harmful psychological effects on both bullies and their victims. Available resources include the *APA Resolution on Bullying Among Children and Youth* (supporting H.R. 1589, the Bullying and Gang Reduction for Improved Education Act of 2009). The APA Web site offers links to a research round-up, bullying prevention programs around the world, and a Getting Help section for adolescents dealing with bullying issues. The association's children's publishing arm, Magination Press, produces e-books such as *Blue Cheese Breath and Stinky Feet* that show young children how to deal with bullies.

American School Counselor Association (ASCA)
1101 King St., Suite 625, Alexandria, VA 22314
phone: (703) 683-2722 • toll-free: (800) 306-4722
fax: (703) 683-1619 • Web site: www.schoolcounselor.org

ASCA promotes professionalism and ethical practices among school guidance counselors and counselors' role in helping students succeed socially as well as academically. The association sponsors workshops such as "Bullying and What to Do About It" and publishes the bimonthly magazine *ASCA School Counselor*. Free online resources include the articles "The Buzz on Bullying" and "Appropriate Use of the Internet." The association's online bookstore offers titles aimed at young people such as *Cool, Calm, and Confident: A Workbook to Help Kids Learn Assertiveness Skills;* anti-bullying posters, banners, and bulletin boards; and sample lesson plans for school-based anti-bullying programs.

Center for Safe and Responsible Internet Use
474 W. Twenty-ninth Ave., Eugene, OR 97405
phone: (541) 556-1145 • e-mail: nwillard@csriu.org
Web site: www.cyberbully.org

The center was founded in 2002 by Nancy Willard, an authority on student Internet use management in schools and the author of *Cyberbullying and Cyberthreats: Responding to the Challenge of Online Social Aggression, Threats, and Distress*. In addition to briefs and guides for educators and parents, the center offers numerous reports, articles, and books for student researchers, including "Sexting and Youth: Achieving a Rational Approach," "Why Age and Identity Verification Will Not Work," and *Cyber-Safe Kids, Cyber-Savvy Teens*.

Centers for Disease Control and Prevention (CDC)
National Center for Injury Prevention and Control
4770 Buford Highway NE, MS F-63, Atlanta, GA 30341-3717
toll-free: (800) 232-4636 • e-mail: cdcinfo@cdc.gov
Web site: www.cdc.gov/ViolencePrevention/youthviolence/schoolviolence/

The CDC is the federal agency responsible for monitoring and responding to public health threats in the United States. It lists physical bullying and social rejection as individual risk factors for youth violence, including school shootings and suicide. It conducts research on the causes, consequences, and prevention of bullying such as the Bullying and Sexual Violence Project and the biannual Student Health and Safety Survey, the results of which are available in numerous reports and guides on the CDC Web site.

Gay, Lesbian, and Straight Education Network (GLSEN)

90 Broad St., 2nd Floor, New York, NY 10004
phone: (212) 727-0135 • fax: (212) 727-0254
e-mail: glsen@glsen.org • Web site: www.glsen.org

Founded in 1990, GLSEN fosters healthy, safe school environments where every student is respected regardless of sexual orientation. It is the oversight organization of more than 4,000 school-based Gay-Straight Alliances (GSAs) and the sponsor of two antidiscrimination school events, the National Day of Silence and No Name-Calling Week. Its antibullying initiatives include the educational Web site ThinkB4YouSpeak.com and the monthly e-newsletter *Respect Report*. The GLSEN Web site offers research reports such as *From Teasing to Torment: School Climate in America; A National Report on School Bullying* and *Shared Differences, The Experiences of Lesbian, Gay, Bisexual, and Transgender Students of Color,* and an anti-bullying toolkit, *New Safe Space Kit*.

Mental Health America

2000 N. Beauregard St., 6th Floor, Alexandria, VA 22311
phone: (703) 684-7722 • toll-free: (800) 273-TALK
e-mail: infoctr@mentalhealthamerica.net
Web site: www.nmha.org

Mental Health America (known from 1909 to 2006 as the National Mental Health Association) is a nonprofit education and advocacy network. The organization works to raise awareness of and end discrimination against mental illness through legislation and the courts, public service announcements, and health insurance reform. Opposing bullying is one aspect of its efforts to improve youth mental health; the organization publishes the fact sheet "Bullying: What to Do About It" and related material on recognizing signs of distress in children, helping children cope with stress, and preventing child and adolescent suicide.

National Center for Bullying Prevention
PACER Center
8161 Normandale Blvd., Bloomington, MN 55437
toll-free: (888) 248-0822 • fax: (952) 838-0199
Web site: www.pacer.org/bullying

Funded by U.S. Department of Education's Office of Special Education Programs, the center is an advocate for children with disabilities and all children subjected to bullying, from elementary through high school. Bullying prevention resources (available in English, Spanish, Hmong, and Somali) include audio-video clips, reading lists, creative writing exercises, group activities, and numerous downloadable handouts such as "Bullying Fast Facts." The center sponsors school and community workshops and events, such as National Bullying Awareness Week each October.

National Crime Prevention Council (NCPC)
2345 Crystal Dr., Suite 500, Arlington, VA 22202
phone: (202) 466-6272 • fax: (202) 296-1356
Web site: www.ncpc.org/topics/cyberbullying

The council, a partnership of the U.S. Department of Justice and private sponsors such as the Wireless Foundation and the Ad Council, was founded in 1979 to get citizens, especially youth, involved in crime prevention. It is best known for televised public service announcements and school-based programs featuring McGruff the Crime Dog. Other novel approaches to addressing social problems include the Community Responses to Drug Abuse and Youth Outreach for Victim Assistance programs. The council's cyberbullying campaign includes a public service ad contest (winning PSAs are viewable on the Web site), free anti-bullying banners users can copy-and-paste into e-mail or social networking pages, the Be Safe and Sound in School program, and educational training manuals for youth and adults to manage bullying and intimidation. Downloadable resources include a range of podcasts and research papers, including the Harris Interactive report/poll *Teens and Cyberbullying*.

Olweus Bullying Prevention Program
Institute on Family & Neighborhood Life
Clemson University
158 Poole Agricultural Center, Clemson, SC 29634-0132
phone: (864) 710-4562 • fax: (406) 862-8971
e-mail: nobully@clemson.edu
Web site: www.clemson.edu/olweus

The program, developed by Norwegian bullying researcher Dan Olweus (ol-VAY-us) in the 1980s, is a school-based intervention program designed to prevent or reduce bullying in elementary, middle, and junior high schools (students six to fifteen years old). It is endorsed as a model anti-bullying program by the Substance Abuse and Mental Health Services Administration (SAMHSA) and the Office of Juvenile Justice and Delinquency Prevention. How the program works, statistical outcomes, and studies of the effectiveness of this and other anti-bullying programs are available at the Web site.

Wired Safety
1 Bridge St., Irvington-on-Hudson, NY 10533
phone: (201) 463-8663 • fax: (201) 670-7002
e-mail: parry@aftab.com •Web sites: www.wiredsafety.org; www.stopcyberbullying.org

Under executive director Parry Aftab, Wired Safety is an Internet safety and help group that offers articles, activities, and advice designed for seven- to seventeen-year-olds on a range of issues including cyberbullying, cyberstalking, and harassment. Resources include a Cyber911 Help Line, a cyberstalking poll, cyberbullying Q&As, and a speakers' bureau. Information available on the Web sites covers Facebook privacy protection, how to handle sexting, building safe Web sites, and many other topics. Wired Safety also sponsors the annual WiredKids Summit on Capitol Hill; in a role reversal, tech-savvy teens get the chance there to present cybersafety research, raise cyberbullying issues, and tell industry and government leaders what they need to know about cybersafety.

Workplace Bullying Institute (WBI)
PO Box 29915, Bellingham, WA 98228
phone: (360) 656-6630
Web site: www.workplacebullying.org

The WBI is a nonprofit organization dedicated to the elimination of workplace bullying through education and research. Founders Gary Namie and Ruth Namie are the authors of *Bullyproof Yourself at Work!* and *The Bully at Work* and sponsors of the Healthy Workplace Bill, introduced in seventeen state legislatures since 2003. Resources available on the WBI Web site include analysis and status updates on the proposed legislation, a research library of more than a hundred journal articles, and industry-specific tools and tutorials for targets of bullying in health care, education, government, and the private sector. The WBI also publishes the e-newsletter *Bully Busters Bytes* and maintains the WBI YouTube channel for educational videos on workplace bullying.

Bibliography

Books

Coloroso, Barbara, *The Bully, the Bullied, and the Bystander: From Preschool to High School*. Updated edition. New York: HarperPaperbacks, 2009.

Guldberg, Helene, *Reclaiming Childhood: Freedom and Play in an Age of Fear*. New York: Routledge, 2009.

Hinjuja, Sameer, and Justin W. Patchin, *Bullying Beyond the Schoolyard: Preventing and Responding to Cyberbullying*. Thousand Oaks, CA: Corwin, 2008.

Kowalski, Robin M., Susan P. Limber, and Patricia W. Agatston, *Cyber Bullying: Bullying in the Digital Age*. Hoboken, NJ: Wiley-Blackwell, 2007.

Lines, Dennis, *The Bullies: Understanding Bullies and Bullying*. London: Jessica Kingsley, 2008.

Meyer, Elizabeth J., *Gender, Bullying, and Harassment*. New York: Teachers College Press, 2009.

Simmons, Rachel, *Odd Girl Speaks Out: Girls Write About Bullies, Cliques, Popularity, and Jealousy*. Orlando, FL: Harcourt, 2004.

Periodicals

Charnock, Elizabeth, "How to Prevent Cyberbullying," *San Francisco Chronicle*, September 2, 2009. http://articles .sfgate.com/2009-09-02/opinion/17204581_1_cyber bullying-electronic-communications-online.

Cumming, Peter, "Children's Rights, Children's Voices, Children's Technology, Children's Sexuality," Speech delivered at Roundtable on Youth, Sexuality, Technology, Joint Session of Association for Research in Cultures of Young People (ARCYP) and Association of Canadian College and University Teachers of English (ACCUTE)

Congress 2009, Carleton University, Ottawa, May 26, 2009. www.liveleak.com/view?i = 4ac_1243736876.

Curier, Joel, "Cyberbullying Emerges as a New Threat," *Seattle Post-Intelligencer*, December 1, 2007. http://seattletimes.nwsource.com/html/nationworld/2004046829_webcyberbully01.html.

Girrbach, Claudia, and Gloria Moskowitz-Sweet, "Kids Deserve Same Protection from Bullying as Adults," San Jose, CA, *Mercury News*, September 20, 2009. www.theopedproject.org/cms/index.php?option = com_content&view = article&id = 182:mn-opinion-kids-deserve-same-protection-from-bullying-as-adults&catid = 38:successes&Itemid = 86.

Griffiths, George Byron, "They've Got His Back," Minneapolis-St. Paul, *Star Tribune*, May 5, 2009. www.startribune.com/opinion/44406997.html?elr = KArksLckD8EQDUoaEyqyP40:DW3ckUiD3aPc:_Yyc:aUUsZ.

Guinther, Chris, "Bullying: It's Not a Rite of Passage," *Southeast Missourian*, April 5, 2009. www.semissourian.com/story/1528007.html.

Hirsch, Afua, "Bullying in the Workplace on the Rise," *Guardian* (Manchester), January 4, 2010. www.guardian.co.uk/money/2010/jan/04/bullying-workplace-recession.

Jacobs, Tom, "How to Turn Your Kid into a Bully," *Miller-McCune*, September 25, 2009. http://miller-mccune.com/news/how-to-turn-your-kid-into-a-bully-1494.

Karlinsky, Neal, and Sidney Wright, "Don't Bully the Bullies, School Learns, Bullies Should Be Treated with Compassion," ABC News.com, March 15, 2009. http://abcnews.go.com/WN/MindMoodNews/Story?id = 7088059&page = 1.

Kazdin, Alan E., and Carlo Rotella, "Bullies: They Can Be Stopped, but It Takes a Village," Slate.com, August 11, 2009. www.slate.com/id/2223976/pagenum/all/#p2.

Klaus, Peggy, "A Sistership of Workplace Infighting," *New York Times,* January 11, 2009. www.nytimes.com/2009/01/11/jobs/11pre.html.

Lisante, Joan E., "Cyberbullying: No Muscles Needed," Connect For Kids, June 3, 2005. www.connectforkids.org/node/3116.

Marshall, Penny, "Generation Sexting: What Teenage Girls Get Up To on the Internet Should Chill Every Parent," *Daily Mail* (London), March 18, 2009. www.dailymail.co.uk/femail/article-1162777/Generation-sexting-What-teenage-girls-really-internet-chill-parent.html.

Mckenna, Phil, "The Rise of Cyberbullying," *New Scientist,* no. 2613, July 19, 2007.

Meese, Mickey, "Backlash: Women Bullying Women at Work," *New York Times,* May 10, 2009. www.nytimes.com/2009/05/10/business/10women.html.

Meyer, Elizabeth, "Why Anti-Bullying Programs Fail to Make School Safer," *Psychology Today,* August 9, 2009. www.psychologytoday.com/blog/gender-and-schooling/200908/why-anti-bullying-programs-fail-make-school-safer.

New York Times, "Vague Cyberbullying Law," September 8, 2009. www.nytimes.com/2009/09/08/opinion/08tue2.html.

Ollove, Michael, "Bullying and Teen Suicide," *Christian Science Monitor,* April 28, 2010.www.csmonitor.com/USA/Society/2010/0428/Bullying-and-teen-suicide-How-do-we-adjust-school-climate.

Paul, Pamela, "Maybe Bullies Just Want to Be Loved," *New York Times,* May 23, 2010. www.nytimes.com/2010/05/23/fashion/23STUDIED.html.

Popkin, Helen A.S., "Cyberbullying Really Is That Bad," MSNBC.com, July 5, 2007. http://today.msnbc.msn.com/id/19620683/ns/technology_and_science_tech_and_gadgets/.

Ruedy, Matthew C., "Repercussions of a MySpace Teen Suicide: Should Anti-Cyberbullying Laws Be Created?" *North Carolina Journal of Law & Technology*, vol. 9, no. 2, Spring 2008. pp. 323–46. http://jolt.unc.edu/sites/default/files/323-346_Ruedy_v9i2.pdf.

Sheehan, Paul, "I Married an Ascham Bully," *Sydney Morning Herald*, May 10, 2009. www.smh.com.au/opinion/i-married-an-ascham-bully-20090510-az41.html?page = -1.

Singh, Neha, and Khin Mai Aung, "A Free Ride for Bullies," *New York Times*, September 23, 2007.

Surdin, Ashley, "In Several States, a Push to Stem Cyber-Bullying: Most of the Laws Focus on Schools," *Washington Post*, December 31, 2008. www.washington post.com/wp-dyn/content/article/2008/12/31/AR 2008123103067.html.

Turley, Jonathan, "How to Punish a Cyberbully," *Los Angeles Times*, November 21, 2007. http://articles.latimes.com/2007/nov/21/news/OE-TURLEY21?pg = l.

Volokh, Eugene, "Federal Felony to Use Blogs, the Web, etc., to Cause Substantial Emotional Distress Through 'Severe, Repeated, and Hostile' Speech?" The Volokh Conspiracy, April 30, 2009. http://volokh.com/posts/1241122059.shtml.

Volokh, Eugene, "Rep. Linda Sanchez Defends Proposed Outlawing of Using Blogs, the Web, etc., to Cause Substantial Emotional Distress Through 'Severe, Repeated, and Hostile Speech,'" The Volokh Conspiracy, May 7, 2009. http://volokh.com/archives/archive_2009_05_03-2009_05_09.shtml#1241740320.

Willard, Nancy E., "The Authority and Responsibility of School Officials in Responding to Cyberbullying," *Journal of Adolescent Health*, 2007. www.jahonline.org/webfiles/images/journals/jah/zaq11207000S64.pdf.

Wiseman, Rosalind, "How to Fight the New Bullies," *Parade*, February 13, 2007. www.parade.com/articles/editions/2007/edition_02-25-2007/Cyberbullying.

Web Sites

Bullying.org (www.bullying.org). This comprehensive site offers FAQs about bullying in school and among peer groups, recent print and online articles, multimedia presentations and Webinars, and an archive of drawings, stories, poems, and music files submitted by young people across North America affected by bullying. The site also recognizes individual young people for noteworthy anti-bullying efforts and has developed a program of activities for a community- or school-based Bullying Awareness Week.

Cyberbullying Research Center (www.cyberbullying .us). A project of Professors Sameer Hinduja of Florida Atlantic University and Justin Patchin of the University of Wisconsin–Eau Claire, the site is a clearinghouse of research and information on the causes and consequences of online harassment. A blog section allows visitors to comment on controversial topics such as whether cyberbullying should be protected as free speech and whether parents should ban computers from teens' bedrooms to reduce cyberbullying. A useful feature for student researchers is the translation of survey results and study statistics into clearly labeled visuals, including numerous downloadable bar graphs.

State and Federal Bullying Information Map, Olweus Bullying Prevention Program (www.olweus.org/public/bullying_laws.page). This site's up-to-date, interactive U.S. map allows users to click on any state for an explanation of that state's laws regarding bullying and harassment, cyberbullying, and hazing. Additional links describe existing and proposed federal laws that mandate bullying and harassment policies and response programs as a condition of federal school funding.

Stop Bullying Now! Campaign, Health Resources and Services Administration, U.S. Department of Health and Human Services (http://stopbullyingnow.hrsa .gov). Divided into "What Kids Can Do" and "What Adults Can Do," this educational site is maintained by the federal government in English and Spanish. On the Kids side, games, quizzes, tips, advice, Webisodes, and question-and-answer pages encourage young people to understand and take a stand against bullying. The Adults side offers advanced resources for high school students, families, and educators.

StopHazing.org (www.stophazing.org). Founded in 1992 at the University of New Hampshire, this site expands anti-bullying topics to oppose hazing practices in high schools and college fraternities and sororities, in athletics, and in the military. The site offers general information and links to laws, myths and facts, speeches, and discussion groups aimed at eliminating hazing; a bulletin board also includes opposing views that defend hazing as harmless.

Index

Picture Credits

About the Editor

Lauri S. Friedman earned her bachelor's degree in religion and political science from Vassar College in Poughkeepsie, New York. Her studies there focused on political Islam. Friedman has worked as a nonfiction writer, a newspaper journalist, and an editor for more than eight years. She has extensive experience in both academic and professional writing settings.

Lauri is the founder of LSF Editorial, a writing and editing business in San Diego. Her clients include Greenhaven Press, for whom she has edited and authored numerous publications on controversial social issues such as oil, the Internet, the Middle East, democracy, pandemics, and obesity. Every book in the *Writing the Critical Essay* series has been under her direction or editorship, and she has personally written more than eighteen titles in the series. She was instrumental in the creation of the series and played a critical role in its conception and development.